Surviving Catholic Ministry

Surviving Catholic Ministry

A Contemporary "Soul of the Apostolate" for the Lay Minister

Brad Bursa

CASCADE *Books* · Eugene, Oregon

SURVIVING CATHOLIC MINISTRY
A Contemporary "Soul of the Apostolate" for the Lay Minister

Cascade Books
An Imprint of Wipf and Stock Publishers
199 W. 8th Ave., Suite 3
Eugene, OR 97401

www.wipfandstock.com

PAPERBACK ISBN: 979-8-3852-2821-8
HARDCOVER ISBN: 979-8-3852-2822-5
EBOOK ISBN: 979-8-3852-2823-2

Cataloguing-in-Publication data:

Names: Bursa, Brad, author.

Title: Surviving Catholic ministry : a contemporary "Soul of the Apostolate" for the lay minister / Brad Bursa.

Description: Eugene, OR: Cascade Books, 2025 | Includes bibliographical references.

Identifiers: ISBN 979-8-3852-2821-8 (paperback) | ISBN 979-8-3852-2822-5 (hardcover) | ISBN 979-8-3852-2823-2 (ebook)

Subjects: LCSH: Lay ministry—Catholic Church. | Spiritual life—Catholic Church.

Classification: BX1920 B87 2025 (paperback) | BX1920 (ebook)

VERSION NUMBER 07/21/25

For KMB

Contents

List of Illustrations

Introduction

Jim etched his rudimentary diagram up on the whiteboard with the chiseled tip of the marker. I lowered my head and cast a final upward glance. He scrawled *live from the inside out* atop the drawing, slanting down to the right. With this, I put my head down, my forehead pressing on the cold, hard table. In an instant, I could see everything that was wrong in my approach to ministry. Actually, I could see everything that was going wrong in my life and in my marriage, too.

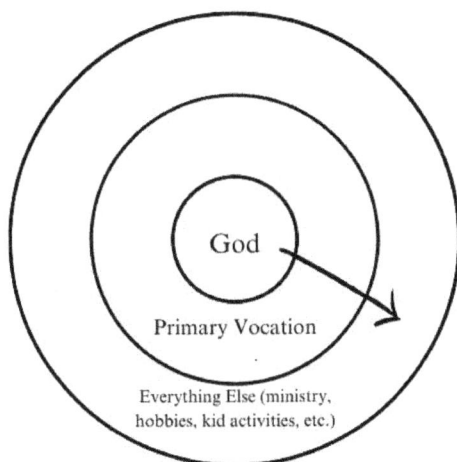

By all appearances, things seemed to be going well for me. About seven years in, my ministry was quite fruitful. We had over three hundred teens involved and over two dozen volunteers. Vocationally, it seemed I was doing well, too. I had been married for seven years and our marriage was fruitful. We had four children, after all.

But rather than living from the inside out, I was doing the exact opposite. This was the sick reality: ministry had become my god. I worshiped it day and night. I spent crazy amounts of time at the church each week trying to figure things out, think up new ideas, reach more teens, and train new volunteers. My family got the leftovers, usually rotten. And God got next to nothing. I had nothing else to give, because when you only give out of yourself, you get empty. I was spent. My marriage was strained. Jesus was no longer my friend, but my job.

As I sat in the workshop for youth ministers with Jim Beckman, I felt as if he shined a light right on the heart of the problem. Jim is a longtime minister, a national speaker, author, and the executive director of the ImpactCenter. His lesson that summer day, drawn from his own experience, turned my world upside down, and inside out.

Jim's concentric circles and "life from the inside out schema" was a modernized rendition of St. Bernard of Clairvaux's twelfth-century lesson on the apostolate. St. Bernard explains:

> "If you are wise, you will be reservoirs and not channels" . . . The channels let the water flow away, and do not retain a drop. But the reservoir is first filled, and then, without emptying itself, pours out its overflow, which is ever renewed, over the fields which it waters. How many there are devoted to works, who are never anything but channels, and retain nothing for themselves, but remain dry while trying to pass on life-giving grace to souls! "We have many channels in the Church today, but very few reservoirs."[1]

---

1. As recounted by Chautard, in *Soul of the Apostolate*, 64–65.

In ministry, we should never get to the point of feeling empty. Often, we think we're instruments in God's hand, and he just wants to "flow" grace through us to other people. We think we're canals. A canal is kind of like a ditch. When it rains, the ditch is full and water flows through it. But that's only when it rains and shortly after. A ditch is usually dry. It's usually empty. In the Christian life, in ministry, we should never be empty. In fact, we can do harm if we're ministering out of ourselves, as if everything depended on us. When we minister this way, depending on our own devices, we dry up and burn out. We can also dry up and burn out others as well.

In place of the canal, we can think of the reservoir, which is always full. The reservoir is always "filled up," and it administers its overflow to water the fields around it. We are called to be spiritual reservoirs. We should only minister out of a place of interior fullness. Ministry is the overflow. Apostolate is the overflow. Jesus came that we might have life and have it to the full (cf. John 10:10). Ministry happens when the "full" spills over. Jim drove St. Bernard's point home with the three circles.

Looking back, I see that workshop as a singular event of grace in my life. Jim convinced me to flip everything around. Really, God did. And he did it through the grace that was flowing from Jim's life into mine. In fact, hearing Jim's talk and trying to put its contents into play likely saved my faith, prevented my marriage from falling apart, and enabled me to stay in ministry. It has been quite the process over the last nine years or so, and this book contains some of what I've learned. Maybe it will help burnt-out ministers start living like reservoirs, start living from the inside out, rather than being dried-up ditches. Maybe it will guide burnt-out ministers toward conversion and they can stay in the field, rather than leaving jaded and frustrated and maybe even bitter.

Burned, Jaded, Gone

I've spoken with so many ministers in the church (clergy and lay) who feel burnt out. Burnout usually involves feeling worn down physically, emotionally, and spiritually. It can happen because a person expends him or herself too much, without replenishment. It's the canal or ditch image being played out in real time. Generally, this is an interior problem. Something needs to change in how the person approaches ministry. But burnout can have exterior causes as well—certain pressures or stressors. When these endure for long periods of time, a person often feels fried. Burnout usually refers to some combination of feeling powerless, worthless, and empty.

To be sure, parish ministry (or diocesan ministry for that matter), is not for the faint of heart. It's hard work. If you take ministry seriously, there's just no way around it. Pick your metaphor for parish work. A lot of the time, you feel as if you're putting out fires or tossing buckets of water out of the sinking Titanic. Anyone bailing out a boat like that is going to get tired. But working hard, even to the point of fatigue, doesn't have to end in burnout.

Jadedness is burnout's blood brother. I think these realities go hand in hand, but jadedness is a deeper spiritual problem. What does it mean to be jaded?

In the late 1400s, the noun "jade" referred to a worn-out horse. A jade was a cart horse who had worked and worked as a beast of burden and could work no more. As a verb, the word appears circa 1600 and it means "to wear out" or "to make dull." This leads into the 1600s, where the adjective appears—to become bored by continual engagement with something.[2] Jadedness is like ennui—dissatisfaction, listlessness, weariness. Most of the people I know who "got burnt out" were straight-up jaded. Burnout usually refers to working too hard for too long. But, I think there is a spiritual component to it and that spiritual part goes by the name "jaded." Anyone who "works for the church" for any amount of time, or who works closely with her ministers, simply knows this to be true. Overworking (or being overworked) is one thing. Being jaded is a horse of a different color. It affects the soul, going beyond mere fatigue. You can hear it in someone's voice. You hear it when most of what they say is disparaging. You hear it when all they do is grumble.

2. Douglas, "Etymology of Jade."

Jadedness prowls under the surface like a cancer. It casts its shadow slowly. Eventually, you diagnose it: "I'm jaded." Jadedness lies a bit deeper than burnout, which you feel more on the surface—usually because *you're exhausted.* The deep-seated origins of jadedness can vary, and the experience is often quite personal. Any jaded minister reading this book may be too close to the causes of his or her jadedness, and many of those causes are ubiquitous in church spaces where it is easy to commiserate and complain.

Burned out people leave ministry. Jaded ones do so bitterly. And, they do so by looking at greener pastures. This makes sense, because when you're burnt out and jaded, everything looks better than your current position.

Rather than encouraging you to flee ministry, this book proposes a different approach to it. It's about turning to Jesus within your circumstances, rather than looking to those of others (i.e., greener pastures) and wishing they were your own.

I have in my mind an image in Fr. Jacques Philippe's book *Searching for and Maintaining Peace* that captures what I'm going after in this book. Philippe argues that we often think peace results from changing our circumstances (i.e., a *freedom from* the constraint we feel or sense in our circumstances). We feel we must change certain things to create a sense of peace for ourselves. Yet, the Christian perspective is precisely the opposite. "It is not the exterior circumstances that must change," Philippe says, "it is above all our hearts that must change."[3] In this case, one begins by discovering Christ within one's circumstances and clinging to him there. Then, circumstances may well change. They also may not. Regardless, I can be at peace because the peace Christ promises is himself, with me, with us, as our all in all (cf. 1 Cor 15:28).

Going a Step Deeper

As I've reflected on Jim's "inside out" image over the last nine years, and attempted to live it, I've come to realize that the point

3. Philippe, *Searching for and Maintaining Peace*, 43.

isn't just a series of external activities. In other words, it's more than praying for a certain amount of time each day and giving God my firstfruits, spending quality time with my family, and then (and only then) pouring into ministry. It's not about only having a weekly date night or only working forty hours a week. It's about something far deeper. Being a reservoir and living from the inside out means living and ministering from a core identity. It means living from a foundational identity as an adopted and beloved son or daughter of God.

Any ministering other than ministering from this place—from this place of being a son or daughter of God—is always going to be fruitless. Without him, we can do nothing (cf. John 15:5). Without being rooted in this fundamental identity as son or daughter and living from the inside out (from that core identity out), without becoming a reservoir of God's love poured out into our hearts by the Holy Spirit (cf. Rom 5:5), we will often wind up empty, jaded, and burnt out.

The plain fact of the matter is this: If you have the foundation right (i.e., identity) and your life is oriented from the inside out (i.e., from interior life into vocation), ministry starts to look different. It occurs from a different, deeper place. You'll find yourself more peaceful and accepting of circumstances—even the more difficult ones.

Audience

I am writing as a Catholic lay minister to my fellow Catholic lay ministers. The term "lay minister" is relatively novel in the life of the Church, emerging in large part since Vatican II. Who is a lay minister, exactly? In a nutshell, a lay minister is one to whom a pastor entrusts a share of the offices and roles connected to his pastoral ministry. However, none of the offices or roles require the character of Orders.[4] I remember my pastor sitting me down when I started in youth ministry and saying something to the effect: "I'm

4. See John Paul II, *Christifideles Laici*, §23.

responsible for all of these people. I need your help in bringing the gospel to the youth—*all* of them."

Now, when a pastor invites a lay person to be a co-worker in carrying out his pastoral ministry, Pope John Paul II says he "ought to acknowledge and foster the ministries, the offices and roles of the lay faithful that find their *foundation in the Sacraments of Baptism and Confirmation,* indeed, for a good many of them, *in the Sacrament of Matrimony.*"[5] Indeed, the roots of lay pastoral ministry run deep, tapping into the grace of baptism and confirmation. But I also want to emphasize that last point, regarding marriage. I'm a married lay minister, so I am writing as a married person who navigates the field as such. The married person brings important perspective to his or her ministry, but also faces unique challenges and juggles significant demands. Consequently, I draw from my experience as a married person throughout this book. I focus heavily on marriage in chapter 3 on primary vocation.

Now, because I'm writing as a lay minister to other lay ministers, and because I'm writing as a married lay minister, does not mean a priest or a lay person who does not carry out an official ministry in the Church won't find value in these pages. Nor does it mean a lay minister who is not married won't find value. The principles I've tried to collate within these pages apply across vocations and roles and situations. The reader can easily and creatively apply the principles. In this way, then, the book is elastic, with applications for those involved in the Church's apostolate when understood in the broadest sense.

A Brief Word on the Title

In ministry-speak, people often talk about not merely surviving, but eventually thriving in ministry. This gets at the movement from barely keeping your head above water to swimming with no problem. It gets at the shift from feeling overwhelmed and

---

5. John Paul II, *Christifideles Laici,* §23.∂

discouraged most (or all) of the time to seeing fruit from your efforts and feeling encouraged by it.

I'm not using "survive" in the same way, here. This isn't a book about bobbing in the ministry waters and catching a breath here and there, so you don't drown. The origins of the word survive have nothing to do with barely hanging on. The word literally means "to live beyond" or "to live longer than." That's the way to understand this book—a series of considerations on how to live longer in ministry and not simply flame out. It's about how to survive by living from a source beyond ministry itself, and, consequently, to be more alive in your ministry.

Disposition

What you have in your hands, then, is not a book about how to do ministry (i.e., a book on methodology). There are plenty of those books, and many of them are very good. Instead, this is a book about how to approach ministry in a way that won't leave you fried. Or, if you're already fried, it's a book that might help you get unstuck: like getting burnt food off the bottom of a pan. It aims to help you get healthy and whole again.

This is a book about disposition—having the right disposition for ministry. Disposition refers to an inclination of heart and mind. It has to do with arranging one's interior in a certain way or opening one's interior life to God. Said another way, this book, then, aims at helping the reader open to God, that God might rearrange his or her life. It has everything to do with conversion. Conversion refers to your whole life being turned around by God—upside down and inside out. It's about the fragments of your life being brought into one and made whole. Conversion is renewal in mind and heart. Such conversion allows for living and ministering from a core identity: as a beloved son/daughter devoted to the interior life, the fruits of which spill into one's vocation, and, finally, into ministry. In some ways, I'd liken this book to a contemporary version of Dom Jean-Baptiste Chautard's classic *The Soul of the Apostolate*. It certainly embraces Chautard's thesis, but in a modern expression, for a particular context (i.e., the lay church worker), and with an emphasis on practical steps one can take to cultivate the right disposition for ministry.

By no means do I claim this short volume exhausts what could be said on this topic. Instead, it's a humble effort that attempts to highlight points of intersection of my experience and the broader theological and spiritual tradition that lends a sense of credibility to my experience.

The Book in Outline

In terms of a structure, the book has a rather simple one. I will first reflect on the need to embrace one's baptismal identity as a son or daughter of God (chapter 1), before moving through the steps for living from the inside out. I will explore establishing the interior life (chapter 2), before turning to primary vocation (chapter 3), and then the impact of this reorganization on our approach to ministry (chapter 4). Finally, I consider the possibility of the need to heal from the wear and tear of ministry and steps one can take toward healing (chapter 5).

I hope this book fosters renewal in your life, in your vocation, and in your ministry. Renewal matters. Once, I heard a priest say, "Renewal has nothing to do with needing the latest Catholic book or a new Catholic show, as great as those things are. It's not about that 'buzz' from a fresh thing or another Catholic event. Instead, it's about rediscovering Christ. It's about recalling that original encounter that you had with him and allowing him to speak to you again." I suppose it's ironic to include his point in a book. But this book is simply a means; it is a means to a greater end. The *end* is Jesus, and the book offers some help for encountering him. Because, when it comes to renewal, encountering Jesus is all that matters. If you do come to encounter Christ again—if you allow him to encounter you—I'm confident you will not only avoid burnout, overcome jadedness, and survive ministry, but you will thrive in the whole of your Christian life.

Identity

I once had a profound stretch of desolation in ministry. It came while I was working at the diocesan level. I had gotten caught up in the bureaucratic machinery. The red tape, the analysis paralysis, and the lack of trust within the institution had brutal effects. For some reason, that which was tremendously fruitful on the parish level was not as fecund at the diocesan one. I was baffled and frustrated. I felt like a failure.

But all of this went deeper than institutional annoyances or personal frustration.

I found myself calling everything into question. The whole brokenness of the Church, the scandal of her humanity oppressed me. "Maybe this is all a fraud," I would think to myself. "Have I just been pulling levers and making things happen? Is this all just a purely human venture? Is it fake? Made up? Man-made? Is God really behind this thing? Is he here?" These are all the same types of thoughts and questions one has in spiritual desolation—but applied to ministry.

I was spinning. Every week I would think about quitting. I drafted numerous resignation letters.

Burdened by this spiritual darkness, my ministry had to keep going like the runaway freight train it often felt like. I was responsible for this and that event. I had scheduled engagements with registered teens; the events needed to be executed out of obligation. I couldn't just quit. I couldn't just not show up. I had to minister to them. I had to speak to them. I had to lead worship. So, I went through the motions. Exteriorly, I looked the ministry part I was supposed to look. Interiorly, I was apathetic, frustrated, and confused. My peace was gone.

I remember sitting at one of the events I was running—a huge, weeklong conference for high school leaders (the disciple-maker types). I was in the chapel listening to a talk given by one of the speakers I brought in. To this day, I cannot remember what she said, but the Spirit was certainly at work. Suddenly, a thought struck me like a lightning bolt: "I don't minister to become a son, but because I am a son."

Instantly, I had a window into the growing source of desolation. Over the years, my ministry became the generator of my fundamental identity. How fruitful I was in ministry determined the degree of my sonship. It is that typical checkbox mentality: God will love me if I _____ (fill in the blank). I was trying to earn God's love through ministry. I was trying to prove my worth.

This is backwards. We don't minister to earn *something* from God or to prove we are *someone*. We minister because *we are someone* in God's eyes. Consequently, we have *something* to give. We are God's adopted sons and daughters. This is our fundamental identity. This changes everything: we know who we are because we know *whose* we are.

Having one's identity in Christ is the premise for the "live from the inside out" approach. The premise is that one has become an adopted son or daughter of God. This is the foundation of the whole thing. This is what makes living from the inside out possible in the first place. Let's consider this identity and how it comes about.

Given a New Identity

Identity refers to the fact of who a person is. It distinguishes this or that individual from others. Identity has to do with finding one's self and identifying with one's self. There's an element of sameness—embracing and accepting who I am as I am.

Identity for the existentialist is something self-created. Existentialism holds that existence precedes essence. Who I am precedes what I am. Existentialism exalts freedom. I am who I make myself out to be. I determine myself, my identity. In this case, identity is in a state of constant flux and ultimately something highly subjective. I make myself.

The Christian view does not discount freedom. But it does not subscribe to such a radically subjective position. Instead, it begins from a relational (and, hence, an objective) one. Personal identity is a relational reality. I find myself, I identify myself, in relation to others. We might think about the foundations of this in terms of creatureliness. I did not make myself. I was created. This implies a Creator, one who made me. Consequently, I find myself set in relation to my Creator from my very origin. Within this relationship, and because of it, I can identify myself as a creature. I am created. Therefore, as a creature whose origin and destiny are outside of myself, or my subjective experience, it makes sense I am always searching outside of myself for an answer to my question about identity.

I'd like to further illustrate my point about finding identity outside of ourselves (i.e., apart from mere self-creation), by sharing a story about one of my children.

My daughter was on the verge of reading, but not quite there yet. My niece had drawn a picture of two of my girls. It hung on the fridge. My daughter, Thérèse, saw it and asked who was pictured.

"That's you, and that's your sister Lilli," I said, pointing to each.

"Nope. Can't be," she replied.

"Well, it is, because I can read. Your name is under this girl, and your sister's name is right here."

"Can't be me," she said.

"Why?" I asked, growing impatient.

"Because you and Mom aren't in the picture," she said, before walking away.

There you have it. That is what it means to be created. Or, more profoundly, that's what it means to be a son or daughter—to be *from* someone constitutes your identity.

Taking all of this one final step further, Christian identity has to do with identifying with Christ. It has to do with "putting on Christ" (cf. Rom 3:14), it has to do with surrendering self-creation, to make myself, and to take on Jesus' identity as the Father's Son. "I live, no longer I, but Christ lives in me" (Gal 2:20). To be a Christian is to become, once again and through grace, a son or daughter of God. To be a son or daughter of God means our whole identity and worth is wrapped up in being created *and* adopted by—being from—God.

Baptismal Identity

In baptism, we are adopted by God as his sons and daughters (CCC §1265). Recall that in the beginning, Adam and Eve were created in God's "image and likeness." They were his created son and daughter in the covenant he established with them. When Adam and Eve fell through their sin, the covenant, the family bond, was broken. They fell out of God's family. The whole of the Old Testament is an account of God's working in the hearts of his people to bring them back into his family through a new and everlasting covenant.

Then, "when the fullness of time had come, God sent his Son, born of a woman, born under the law, to ransom those under the law, so that we might receive adoption. As proof that you are children, God sent the spirit of his Son into our hearts, crying out, 'Abba, Father!'" (Gal 4:4–6). When we were baptized, "we were indeed buried with him through baptism into death, so that, just as Christ was raised from the dead by the glory of the Father, we too might live in newness of life" (Rom 6:4). We no longer identify with our sin, but we identify with him. Our being created in God's "image and likeness," and the restoration of this sonship or daughterhood in baptism, is the truth of our identity and the source of our worth. Therefore, we never tire of hearing that beautiful line from Pope John Paul II: "*We are not the sum of our weaknesses and failures*; we are the sum of the Father's love for us and our real capacity to become the image of his Son."[1] Baptism unites us to Christ in his sonship, in his perfect self-offering to the Father. We become sons and daughters *in the Son*. The *Catechism* explains, the Father "has caused us to be reborn to his life by adopting us as his children in his only Son: by Baptism, he incorporates us into the Body of his Christ" (§2782).

Adoption is parenthood by choice. To be sure, there's a choice involved in biological parenthood as well, but it is a choice to be open to the possibility of a life *given* to the husband and wife—father and mother. In adoption, parents see the person, the child. They see the good and (in some cases) the bad; they see a child who has a history outside their own. That history might be a dark one. In adoption, the adoptive parents see the child and love the child and choose the child anyway. The child is given over to another and to others (i.e., the family). The child is reborn—given a new set of relationships, a new start, a new beginning. The child receives a new family and is incorporated into it, and the child is given a new identity.

God's adopting us means God choosing us. This is wild when you think about it. Our deepest desire as human beings has to do with being seen—with being seen, known, and loved. Psychology confirms this. For example, Dr. Matthew Brueninger explains that we have a central relational paradox that we want close relationships, we want to be liked, but we're afraid we won't be liked. Said another way, we desperately want to be seen, but we also want to remain hidden, because if someone saw us as we really are, that person could leave. This is the paradox: we want to be seen, and we want to hide.[2] And, here comes God, who sees perfectly, who sees us as we really are (i.e., as sinners) and chooses us anyway—to the point of dying for us (cf. Rom 5:8).

To receive the sacrament of baptism is to receive a new identity. Now, I am neither what I make of myself, nor what the world says I am. Instead, I am You who loves me. I am a son (or daughter

1. John Paul II, "Homily—17th World Youth Day (July 28, 2002)."
2. See Brueninger interview in Johnson, dir., *My Father's Father*.

in the case of females) in the Son. I can love and accept myself with the love that Christ has shown me. It's not a love that dismisses sin, but which sees me, the person, and forgives that which mars the image. It's a love that calls me to become who I am. This love transforms identity: "I live, no longer I, but Christ lives in me" (Gal 2:20). Baptism makes this encounter with Christ possible. Baptism generates this new identity. In other words, it's not something I simply will for myself, some sort of subjective exercise. No. The Christian event is an objective event. All this becomes clear in the next chapter of Galatians, where Paul goes on to say: "For through faith you are all children of God in Christ Jesus. For all of you who were baptized into Christ have clothed yourselves with Christ" (Gal 3:26–27). In baptism, the objective encounter with Christ happens to us. In baptism, we are adopted as sons and daughters, we are given over to God and incorporated into the body of Christ, the church. We are given a new family. We are given a new identity: sons and daughters of God.

In baptism, we are adopted. In baptism, we are given an irrevocable identity. In baptism, we become sons and daughters of God. This identity, grounded in relationship, means I identify with the other, with God. I am who I am because of *whose* I am. I know who I am because I know *whose* I am. I am who I am because I know the One from whom my dignity comes. And he sees me and knows me.

Spoken to Us, Too

When we are baptized, we are baptized into Jesus Christ, the Son of God who was baptized into our humanity. Jesus immersed himself into the human condition, like us in all things but sin (cf. Heb 4:15). Though he did not sin, he took on, himself, the full weight of the effects of sin: "For our sake he made him to be sin who did not know sin, so that we might become the righteousness of God in him" (2 Cor 5:21). The Gospel writers recount this immersion in the scene of the baptism of the Lord. Pope Benedict XVI offers the following commentary on this scene:

> Jesus loaded the burden of all mankind's guilt upon his shoulders; he bore it down into the depths of the Jordan. He inaugurated his public activity by stepping into the place of sinners. His inaugural gesture [baptism in the Jordan] is an anticipation of the Cross . . . The Baptism is an acceptance of death for the sins of humanity, and the voice that calls out "This is my beloved Son" over the baptismal waters is an anticipatory reference to the Resurrection.[3]

After his baptism, as Jesus prayed, we hear that "heaven was opened and the holy Spirit descended upon him in bodily form like a dove. And a voice came from heaven, 'You are my beloved Son; with you I am well pleased'" (Luke 3:21–22). These words are meant for us, too. The logic flows like this: if we when we are baptized, are baptized into Christ and become sons and daughters in the Son, then what the Father speaks to the Son, he speaks to us. When you and I were baptized, it's as if God whispered these words that need to echo throughout the whole of our lives: "You are my beloved son. With you I am well pleased." "You are my beloved daughter. With you I am well pleased."

At Home in the Love of God

When I think of abiding in my baptismal identity, I think of staying "home" in the Lord. Here's what I mean. In the first chapter of John's Gospel, we hear that John the Baptist is standing with his disciples when Jesus walks by. John lets them know that this is the Lamb of God. Two of John's disciples start following Jesus, who takes notice. He turns and asks them what they are looking for. (As an aside, it's important to note that the first words on Jesus' lips in John's Gospel are a question: "What are you looking for?" It's a question about desire. Jesus takes our desires seriously.) The disciples of John the Baptist respond rather clumsily: "Where are you staying?"

---

3. Benedict XVI, *Jesus of Nazareth*, 18.

Regarding the clumsiness, I often wonder if their principal answer is implied: "You! We have been on the lookout for the Lamb of God, for the Messiah. We have been longing for you." So, they want to know where he's staying because they don't want to leave him.

Jesus responds with an invitation: "Come and you will see." So, they go and stay with him. Now, this should raise a question. Where did they go? Earlier in the chapter, we hear that Jesus, the Word, took flesh and dwelt among us—made his abode, his home among us (cf. John 1:15). Jesus is here, with us. Therefore, the literal meaning of the text indicates that they went to a physical location on the face of the earth.

However, we can go deeper into a spiritual understanding. In John 1:18, we read that "No one has ever seen God. The only Son, God, who is at the Father's side, has revealed him." With this verse in mind, where is the Son? *He is at the Father's side.* He is in the bosom, in the heart of the Father (the Greek word used here is *kolpos*). Jesus abides in the heart of the Father; he is one with the Father. The Son rests his head on the heart of the Father, allowing the heartbeat of the Father to be the beat of his own life. Jesus' life moves according to the rhythm of the Father's heart. When Jesus invites the two disciples of John the Baptist to "come and see," he shows them the heart of the Father.

Now, if you fast forward in John's Gospel to the thirteenth chapter, we learn that after Jesus washed the disciples' feet, the beloved disciple rested his head on the *kolpos* of Jesus. In so many ways, the beloved disciple represents every disciple throughout the Gospel. We're all God's beloved disciples. And, here, the beloved disciple models the proper posture for a disciple—abiding in, resting in the heart of Jesus. Our lives are to move according to the beat of Jesus' heart.

If you use your imagination for a moment to visualize something, I think we can round out the image. If the beloved disciple (you!) is resting his head on the heart of Jesus, and Jesus is resting his head on the heart of the Father, then where is the beloved disciple positioned? *Between the hearts of the Father and the Son.* By the way, I'm pretty sure this is what life in the Spirit is all about. It's about abiding in the Love of the Father and Son, the Love between Father and Son. That Love is the Holy Spirit.

Whenever my wife and I give each other a hug, our daughter, Cécile, seems to come out of nowhere and wedge herself between us. She looks up at us with her big eyes and says: "My home." There's something wonderfully endearing about this childlike act. There's also something insightful. When applied to the image of abiding between the hearts of the Father and Son from John's Gospel, we, too, can spiritually say: "My home." Jesus made his home with us, that we might make our home in God—and abide in it. To abide in our baptismal identity is to be at home in the Lord.

Be Yourself; Teach Yourself

Being at home in the Lord provides you with the security necessary to be yourself and to witness to Christ through your very person.

My first year of teaching was a blur. I think this is the case for most first-year teachers. It's just overwhelming, like drinking from a firehose. I don't remember many of the details from that year, but I do know, taken as a whole, it was an intensely formative one. While I don't remember many specifics, one memory has stuck with me and still radically impacts everything I do in ministry. Here's the story.

My seventh bell, the last class each day, was my biggest class. By that time of day, there were thirty sophomores who wanted nothing more than to get out of the school building. Quite honestly, I did too. These were not the kids you'd find at the top of the class rankings. So, by the time they got to me, they were mentally checked out. This was all compounded by the fact that I knew nothing about classroom management. I had no idea how to control a bunch of rowdy, spent sophomores. I wasted a lot of time trying to figure out the right lesson plan, the right approach to get something across. The execution was lacking. As the weeks wore on, I was feeling a shell of myself. Beaten down, I dreaded the seventh bell every day.

Luckily, Marc smoked at the time. Marc was my mentor teacher. Sometimes we would take rides during our overlapping free bell—the sixth of the day. He would smoke. I would smoke secondhand. His Subaru Forester created the perfect mobile smoking lounge. It calmed me down.[4]

One day, I was sharing about this dreaded seventh bell and all of my failed attempts to teach my students something. He must have sensed I was at my wit's end.

He looked at me and said (I can still see him inhaling and then exhaling the smoke through his teeth as he talked), "You know, these kids aren't going to remember most of what you tell them."

"Well then, why am I wasting my time doing this?" I retorted.

He repeated himself, "These kids aren't going to remember most of what you tell them. But, they will remember you. So, teach yourself."

It was Marc's way of saying: be yourself in the classroom.

He went on, "It's not about being egotistical. It's about letting them come to know who God is through you and how God is moving in your life. They need to see how God has shaped your personality."

Be yourself. Teach yourself. I took this as my marching order for seventh bell (and all the other bells). And, I carried it right into parish ministry. Be yourself. Teach yourself. And let them see through you to the One you're teaching about, the One who shaped your being. Let them see through you to Jesus himself.

The Saint as a Window

Joseph Ratzinger has a beautiful teaching about sainthood that moves down the same path and further illustrates my friend Marc's point.[5] By "sainthood" here, Ratzinger means something like St. Paul's reference to the Christians of the early church. For Paul, the

4. Please note that I am not recommending smoking as a solution for poor classroom management skills. I'm just setting the scene.

5. I will refer to Joseph Ratzinger or Pope Benedict XVI according to his title at the time the cited piece was written.

word did not denote only those canonized, or even canonizable Christians. The word "saint" does not refer to "a headlong leap into heroism," or "adventurous achievements of virtue."[6] Instead, the word refers to Christ's own sanctifying initiative and action that sanctifies the church and her members. It refers to those "saints" who "with Jesus receive a ray of his brightness" and who are "called to use their experience of the risen Lord to become a point of reference for others that could bring them into contact with Jesus' vision of the living God."[7] The saints are witnesses; they are reference points or living windows that allow the light of Christ, the living God, to reach others. We are all called to be saints. I am called to be one. You are, too. You and I are called to radical transformation in Christ, such that when you're teaching yourself, you're preaching Christ.

The image of a stained-glass window captures all of this magnificently. Stained glass consists of thousands of fragments fitted together. Without light illuminating it, stained glass is unintelligible. When you're in a church at night, the jet-black panels are portals of darkness. Hard. Cold.

But, in the morning, the sunlight touches each of those pieces of glass—suddenly illuminating the whole of it and fitting each piece into a mosaic of color. Suddenly the window makes sense. The stained-glass window itself is a testimony to the light that illuminates it—it refers to the light, so to speak. So it is for the saint. So it is with us. We need the light of Christ to touch the fragments of our lives and make us whole. We need the light to bring the whole thing into focus. When this happens, we become capable of being reference points to that light everywhere we go. This is what it means to live our identity and to allow the source of it to shine for all to see (cf. Matt 5:16).

---

6. Ratzinger, *Yes of Jesus Christ*, 104–5. See also Benedict XVI, "Holiness." We could also queue up Pope Paul VI in *Evangelii nuntiandi* §41: "Modern man listens more willingly to witnesses than to teachers, and if he does listen to teachers, it is because they are witnesses."

7. Ratzinger, *Yes of Jesus Christ*, 30–33.

Staying Above the Snake Line

When one steps into a ministry role, one is stepping onto the battlefield. To be sure, the whole of the Christian life is a battle (cf. CCC §409). But you really come under attack when you set out to evangelize, to catechize, and to save souls. It turns out, staying above the snake line makes the difference in this battle. And rooting ourselves in our baptismal identity is the key to remaining above the snake line.

Snakes crawl on their bellies, low to the ground. Scraping the earth. They dwell in low areas, awaiting their prey, ready to pounce. In the mountains and regions high above sea level, one does not find snakes. These low-lying creatures do not like altitude, they cannot withstand the elements of the heights. They remain below a certain line. This is the invisible "line," a certain altitude, above which you will not find snakes and below which you will. People refer to this phenomenon as the "snake line."

Beyond camping or hiking, we can apply the snake line to spiritual matters. For in our spiritual lives, we should strive to remain above the snake line. We are to avoid those base areas of temptation, those valleys of secretive darkness, and the confusion caused by self-doubt. Below the snake line, lying in wait, we find the devil, "a murderer from the beginning," who "does not stand in truth, because there is no truth in him. When he tells a lie, he speaks in character, because he is a liar and the father of lies" (John 8:44). He is the accuser, *diabolos,* one who rips apart and tears asunder.

Identity crises, that is forgetting we are beloved sons and daughters of God, often lie at the heart of our dip beneath the snake line. When this happens, we are susceptible to attack. Our forgetfulness of our identity, our lack of awareness of communion with God, is an apt description of concupiscence, that inclination to sin that remains even after original sin is washed away in baptism. In the fall, the *Catechism* says, "Man, tempted by the devil, let his trust in his Creator die in his heart and, abusing his freedom, disobeyed God's command. This is what man's first sin consisted of. All subsequent sin would be disobedience toward God and *lack of trust in his goodness"* (§397). Concupiscence is tied to original sin. Original sin was not an outright rejection of God, but a break in filial relationship with him. In the original sin, Adam and Eve stopped believing that God was their loving Father and they stepped out of relationship. They had fallen below the snake line, jeopardizing and eventually losing the sense of their identity.

God calls us to remain above the snake line. "Remain in my love," he says (John 15:9). It's as if he's saying, "Hold fast to your identity as my son. Hold fast to your identity as my daughter. Don't forget that I see you, that I know you, that I've chosen you. I adopted you. You are mine."

Once, I was asked to give a retreat to more than 100 Catholic school principals in my diocese. I accepted, but with hesitation. The whole thing made me incredibly anxious. I mean, who wants to speak to 100-plus principals? I suppose some people do, but I don't. And I didn't then. As I was driving to the retreat, I found myself under constant attack. I had fallen well beneath the snake line. I was being ruthlessly accosted. Intense feelings of self-doubt, lies, accusations, and so forth flowed through my mind. It was overwhelming. Numerous times I almost turned around. I think I even picked up my phone to call in sick. I can't quite remember because of the mental anguish.

About five miles from the retreat site, God's light broke into my darkness (cf. John 1:5). In an instant, I had a deep awareness of his love and of my identity. I thought to myself, "If they hate me or what I have to say, nothing changes in my relationship with God. If they don't listen or dismiss me, God still loves me. If they reject me, God doesn't. I am still his beloved son. This is the only thing that matters." God brought me above the snake line. He picked me up and carried me right back to that spiritual home in his heart and all the dark thoughts that had overwhelmed me for nearly an hour were gone. I was able to offer the retreat in confidence and in freedom. This experience, however brief, was a lesson in staying above the snake line. To stay above it, you must root yourself in your identity as a beloved son or daughter of God. Allow God to remind you of this identity and claim it. Simple as that.

Conclusion

Baptism initiates us into life in Christ as adopted sons and daughters of God. We are thus given a new identity and God sets our life on a new trajectory. Gone are the days of self-creation. Gone are the days of self-assertion. Broadly speaking, the new trajectory, the decisive direction of life moves from inside out. We're talking about a new relational horizon, no longer limited to or eclipsed by the self. It's a horizon grounded in relationship with God and moving outward from there to relationship with others (and, inevitably, back in again). Next, I will dig into cultivating the interior life, such that God can plant seeds and water them and they bear fruit throughout the whole of one's life.

—— 2 ——

Interior Life

J esus doesn't mince his words in John's Gospel: "Without me you can do nothing" (John 15:5). Without abiding in him, without rooting ourselves in him, without identifying with him, we can do nothing. In other words, we must abide in our baptismal identity in order to bear fruit.

How do we abide? How is the disciple to remain in his love amid the tug and pull of life, a hundred thousand things trying to distract and drag us away?

The answer is simple: by building up the interior life. By "interior life," I mean the same as Chautard does in *The Soul of the Apostolate*. For Chautard, interior life is not merely that gift of divine life, that spiritual interiority given to us by sanctifying grace in baptism. Instead, Chautard uses the expression with regard to "the actual interior life." He's talking about that movement from potency to act, from the real potential for an interior life to the actualizing of it. He says, "I can define it as the state of activity of a soul which strives against its natural inclinations in order to *regulate* them, and endeavors to acquire the *habit* of judging and directing its movements *in all things* according to the light of the Gospel."[1] An active interior life involves a twofold movement, according to Chautard. First, the person withdraws from all

1. Chautard, *Soul of the Apostolate*, 28. Emphasis in original.

that is opposed to God, thus attaining a sense of being recollected. Second, the "soul tends upwards to God, and unites itself with Him."[2] Said another way, the growth in the interior life refers to "conversion of the heart, interior conversion" (CCC §1430).

How does one *actualize* the interior life, this inheritance given him or her in baptism?

Amongst other means (e.g., the sacraments, a life of virtue, etc.), I can say with confidence that prayer actualizes the interior life. Indeed, as the *Catechism* says, "Prayer is the life of the new heart. It ought to animate us at every moment" (CCC §2697). Therefore, the first step in Jim Beckman's schema of living from the inside out has to do with building up the interior life, grounding our lives in the fundamental baptismal identity, through prayer.

Prayer: The Disciple's First Mission

In Mark 3:13–19 (cf. Luke 6:12–16), the evangelist recounts the calling of the apostles. Mark introduces this account by noting that Jesus "went up the mountain." Throughout Scripture, mountains often indicate closeness with God. Luke is more explicit in this regard, saying that Jesus went to the mountain and spent the whole night in prayer (Luke 6:12). Pope Benedict XVI reflects on this scene:

> The calling of the disciples is a prayer event; it is as if they were begotten in prayer, in intimacy with the Father. The calling of the Twelve, far from being purely functional, takes on a deeply theological meaning: Their calling emerges from the Son's dialogue with the Father and is anchored there ... You cannot make yourself a disciple— it is an event of election, a free decision of the Lord's will, which in its turn is anchored in his communion of will with the Father.[3]

---

2. Chautard, *Soul of the Apostolate*, 28.
3. Benedict XVI, *Jesus of Nazareth*, 170.

We do not make ourselves disciples by our own power. God initiates. Discipleship is borne from the prayer of the Son—from his dialogue with the Father. The Father desires our discipleship. It originates not in our own willing, but in God's willing.

By way of a second point, Benedict XVI notes that the Twelve are tasked with a dual responsibility: being *with* him and being *sent* by him to preach with authority (cf. Mark 3:13–15). At first glance, the dual mission seems to be contradictory: being-with and being-sent is like saying, "Stay here. Go away." In response, Pope Benedict XVI says:

> Jesus appoints the Twelve with a double assignment: "to be with him, and to be sent out to preach." They must be with him in order to get to know him; in order to attain that intimate acquaintance with him that could not be given to the "people"—who saw him only from the outside and took him for a prophet, a great figure in the history of religions, but were unable to perceive his uniqueness (cf. Mt 16:13–ff). The Twelve must be with him so as to be able to recognize his oneness with the Father and thus become witnesses to his mystery . . . One might say that they have to pass from outward to inward communion with Jesus.[4]

The "being with" is distinctly described here in terms of an intimate knowledge that sees in Jesus what the "people" could never see. Being *with* Jesus means coming to know Jesus, as if from the inside. In this sense, it is proper to identify the disciple as the witness. Benedict describes the disciples as those who become witnesses to his mystery, namely his oneness with the Father. Discipleship requires witnessing, and for one to be a witness, he or she must have firsthand experience or direct knowledge of the event. In this case, we are talking about a firsthand experience or knowledge of the Christian event—Jesus Christ. In being *with* Jesus the disciples *see* Jesus, and in seeing Jesus, they *see* God (cf. John 14:9). The disciple, then, is one who is called by the Father through Jesus Christ to intimately know the Father through Jesus Christ. The disciple is

---

4. Benedict XVI, *Jesus of Nazareth*, 172.

to remain *with* Jesus always. It's a foundational, enduring mission, such that even as one is *sent* by Jesus on mission, that one remains *with* him.

But, how does the witness actually come to see, or to know, intimately, this Jesus? How does one remain forever with Jesus? Benedict XVI answers this question by noting that the disciple, the one who sees Jesus from the inside and not the outside, sees him *at prayer*. Gospel passages that speak of Jesus withdrawing to pray, "give us a glimpse into Jesus' filial existence, into the source from which his action and teaching and suffering sprang. This 'praying' of Jesus is the Son conversing with the Father."[5] However, there is more. The one called by Jesus, the disciple, not only witnesses Jesus pray, as if from a distance (e.g., in the agony in the garden), but enters into Jesus' prayer.

Elsewhere, Ratzinger explains that this is the way one comes to know the Son most intimately: from the inside. He says, "Only by entering into Jesus' solitude, only by participating in what is most personal to him, his communication with the Father, can one see what this most personal reality is; only thus can one penetrate to his identity [see his face]. This is the only way to understand him and to grasp what 'following Jesus' means."[6] He clarifies this further, saying, "Since the center of the person of Jesus is prayer, it is essential to participate in his prayer if we are to know and understand him."[7]

The "being with" or "witnessing" that is inherent in discipleship is, in essence, nothing short of an entry through, with, and in the Son and his communication with the Father. Here, the disciple learns who God is and what love is. In Jesus' prayer, "Jesus' human consciousness and will, his human soul, is taken up into that exchange [of love], and in this way human 'praying' is able to become a participation in this filial communion with the Father."[8] Discipleship, in this sense, has its origin in the Son's prayer, and

5. Benedict XVI, *Jesus of Nazareth*, 7.
6. Ratzinger, *Behold the Pierced One*, 19.
7. Ratzinger, *Behold the Pierced One*, 25.
8. Benedict XVI, *Jesus of Nazareth*, 7.

prayer, as the first mission of the disciple, is a participation in the Son's prayer.

Jesus reiterates the same point in the Martha and Mary account (see Luke 10:38–42, for example). In this story, Martha complains to Jesus (her house guest!) that Mary is not helping with the table service. Instead, Mary is sitting at Jesus' feet, listening. Jesus says Mary has chosen the better part and it will not be taken away. Now, Jesus does not denounce Martha's activity. He simply points out the need for a prior given, a foundational posture, and it is one of prayer, of listening to God. Mary was abiding in Jesus, while Martha had practically forgotten him in her effort to serve him. Her activism blinded her.

The disciples, yes, they are called to be sent, but they are only effective as long as they abide in Jesus. So, too, most of us are called to be Marthas, busying ourselves with cultivating the kingdom of God on earth, but this is only effective insofar as we are first (and always) Marys. Without prayer—the interior life—as the enduring foundation of our ministry, we risk falling into what Dom Chautard, in *The Soul of the Apostolate,* calls the "heresy of good works."[9] This heresy consists of feverish activity that might begin from God before forgetting him entirely with the good work inserted in his place. It devolves into idol worship, that is, worshiping what we ourselves are doing and have done.

Prayer: A Marian Posture

Let's talk about a different Mary for just a moment—Mary, the mother of God. Mary maintains intimacy with God throughout the whole of her life. We get glimpses of this in the annunciation, in the notes about Mary holding certain things, pondering them in her heart, and at the cross. She remains close to Jesus physically,

9. Chautard, *Soul of the Apostolate,* 25. Chautard explains that the apostle who looks "only to his own personal activity and talents" as the basis for apostolic success, whose feverish activity takes the place of God, whose ignorance of grace and exercise of human pride, is the one advancing this heresy.

but also with a certain interiority. Mary is a model of prayer for us, and we can consider her life a "school of prayer."

Mary is the preeminent icon of the Church. The *Catechism* says, "By her complete adherence to the Father's will, to his Son's redemptive work, and to every prompting of the Holy Spirit, the Virgin Mary is the Church's model of faith and charity" (CCC §967). She models intimacy with Christ.

The Catholic tradition recognizes certain "dimensions" of the Church. Most fundamentally, we might think of a mystical dimension and a hierarchical one. To this duality, we could also add a missional one, for example. These dimensions have certain figures associated with them: Mary, Peter, and Paul, respectively. Hierarchy contains structures within it. In terms of ministry, we can think of all the organizational and programmatic aspects. This mode of organizing and ranking priorities has a kind of Petrine ring to it. The Pauline dimension of ministry is that lively activity and outreach. But neither the Petrine nor Pauline dimensions of the Church (or of our ministries) have any verve without interiority, without holiness. For this reason, the Church holds:

> "[The Church's] structure is totally ordered to the holiness of Christ's members. And holiness is measured according to the 'great mystery' in which the Bride responds with the gift of love to the gift of the Bridegroom." Mary goes before us all in the holiness that is the Church's mystery as "the bride without spot or wrinkle." This is why the "Marian" dimension of the Church precedes the "Petrine" (CCC §773).

By prioritizing the interior life in the movement from the inside out, we are entering into the Marian dimension of the Church, this enduring precedent on which everything structural or missional hangs and toward which it is ordered.

What Is Prayer?

In a nutshell, prayer is a loving conversation. It's a conversation with the God who loves you. It's a conversation with God in love.

Peter Kreeft explains how natural this should be: "Can you talk to a friend? Then you can talk to God, for he is your Friend. And that is what prayer is . . . Prayer is so simple that no method at all is needed."[10] It's not a matter of a right formula or doing this to get that. It's not mechanistic. It's not a matter of technique. God is not a divine robot we are trying to program a certain way so as to get him to do something for us. Prayer is about love—loving conversation.

Now, a conversation involves speaking and listening. Listening is perhaps the most critical element of any good conversation. If there's no listening, a dialogue devolves into a monologue. In prayer, we talk *and* listen to the Lord. And, listening is most critical. Kreeft puts it this way:

> In a conversation, if you are the wisest, it makes sense for you to do most of the talking. If the other person is wiser, it makes sense for you to do most of the listening . . . Well, prayer is conversation with God, and it makes no sense for us to do most of the talking. We ought to be listening most of the time.[11]

Why Pray?

In short, we pray because prayer is what we were made from and what we are made for. In Genesis 1:26–27, we hear:

> Then God said: Let us make human beings in our image, after our likeness. Let them have dominion over the fish of the sea, the birds of the air, the tame animals, all the wild animals, and all the creatures that crawl on the earth. God created mankind in his image; in the image of God he created them; male and female he created them.

The persons of Trinity are in a trialogue—they're having a conversation *as* God. And, God is love (1 John 4:8). So, the persons of the Trinity are having a conversation in love. In a sense, they are praying.

10. Kreeft, *Prayer for Beginners*, 25.
11. Kreeft, *Prayer for Beginners*, 33.

And, what are they praying about? They're praying about us. They're praying about making us in their image and likeness.

It's worth stopping to think about what this means for a few minutes. What does it mean that human beings are made in and are to be the image and likeness of God? We can get at an answer in at least two ways. First, we ought to note that after Genesis 1, we next see those words "image and likeness" in Gen 5:3. This verse says, "Adam was one hundred and thirty years old when he begot a son in his likeness, after his image; and he named him Seth." Based on contextual evidence, then, we see that "image and likeness" refers to filiation, to sonship—Adam and Eve were the *created* sons and daughters of God. As such, they were God-like. An image points to that which it images—it refers to it—like a child's very being points to his or her parents. Our idiom that a child is a "spitting image" of the parents is indicative of this.

We should also note that ancient Hebrew—the language the Bible was first written in—is an active and nonabstract language. Image denotes the reality as present. This is why the Israelites could not have images or statues. Crafting a statue is an act of idolatry because the statue would somehow contain the reality. We have no problem saying I'm not praying to the statue, but to whom the statue represents. In ancient Israel, this was not possible. The Hebrew word for "image" is *selem*. This denotes "function." It has to do with carrying out a function. The Greek word for "image" is *ikon*, which denotes presence. To be made in God's "image" means the human being contains the function (what God does) and the reality/presence (who God is). So, if Genesis uses the word "image" for man, it is being decisive and precise. It's to say God's "function" (what God does) and his "presence" was in man. In other words: Man participates in the divine. He has within himself a divine "spark," a divine "presence." The human being mediates God's presence in the created order.

Human beings are that part of God's creation that stand in a unique relationship to him. We participate in creation as God's image within it. We are God's children, borne from his prayer—who participate in his own conversation through our own conversation with him. In this way, we see prayer in both our origin and our destiny. We were made from prayer and for prayer.

We are made for prayer—to communicate, to be in communion with God for all eternity. Prayer corresponds with my destiny. When I pray, I get a foretaste of eternity. Prayer propels me towards fulfilling my purpose or destiny: sainthood. Sainthood is simply eternal life with God. We are all called to be saints, so we are all called to pray. Kreeft echoes this, when he says:

> Prayer is necessary because without it we cannot attain *the meaning of life, the end and purpose of our existence.* Becoming saints is the meaning of life . . .It is why God created us . . .[All of God's stupendous effort in salvation history] was for one end: to make saints, to make little Christs, to give his Son brothers and sisters. The whole universe is a saint-making machine. And prayer is the fuel that powers it . . . Prayer is the first step in becoming saints. The second step is charity, a life of love, the ecstasy of giving ourselves away over and over again forever, as each of the Persons of the Trinity do. But this is prayer too, or the extension of prayer.[12]

When we pray, we remember our origin and anticipate our destiny. When we pray, then, we *really* live. When we pray, right now, we abide with the God who is our origin and our destiny—we participate in God's communication that he shares with us. We abide in God who wants us to have life and have it abundantly (cf. John 10:10).

Relationships depend on communication. Friendships fall apart without it. A husband and a wife who don't talk don't last as a couple. Quality time and quality conversation matters. Relationships depend on communication, like the body depends on oxygen. So, too, prayer gives life to the soul and one's relationship with God depends on it. Really, the fulfillment of one's purpose in life depends on it, too, as Fr. Michael Scanlan points out: "If we don't pray I don't think we can ever get our lives in order or accomplish all we are called upon to accomplish. Whether you are

12. Kreeft, *Prayer for Beginners*, 23–24.

a father or mother, husband or wife . . . prayer is what brings your life together."[13] Prayer is what makes you whole, and holds all the pieces of life and parts of you together. If we come from prayer and exist for prayer, then prayer is the most natural thing we can do.

The Danger of Leaving Prayer Behind

During my first year of parish youth ministry, I somehow got introduced to an atheistic eighteen-year-old. The kid was wicked smart and I was bound and determined to convince him of God's existence. We decided to meet weekly for discussion and frequently emailed thoughts and questions between. Since I am an achiever who does not do well when things remain incomplete, this was a recipe for disaster.

As the conversation wore on and I seemed to be getting nowhere, I decided it might help if I understood his position better. So, I entered the dark world of Internet atheism. I watched YouTube videos of prominent atheists and read blog posts. I even read the comments on blogs and social media posts. I got in deep.

Amid this determined effort, my wife and I had our first baby, which upended all of my normal prayer routines. There I was, overwhelmed on all sides of life, frustrated by the atheist, immersing myself in atheistic literature, and not praying.

I could feel my faith slipping. I had unplugged from God and plugged into atheism. I could no longer hear God's voice in my life. It was so bad, that one day I sent a text to my spiritual director that was something like: "I think I'm an atheist."[14] Within five minutes, he had called me. I explained to him what was going on. He listened. Patiently. Then, with the full force of his voice reverberating through the phone, he practically shouted: "Brad, you know *Jesus.* You *know* Jesus. Brad, *you* know Jesus."

His words struck like lightning. I was stunned.

13. Scanlan, *Appointment with God*, 3.

14. In all reality, I had not become an atheist youth minister. I was, however, thinking like an atheist.

I did know Jesus. And, I had been following Jesus because he had been good to me for so many years. I had forgotten this and slowly I was removing all those tethers to this memory, this central fact on which my life rested. I had dismantled the spiritual supports, the most significant of which was daily prayer. After calling *the* thing to mind, my spiritual director put the supports back in place and got me on solid footing. I began praying again.

I learned the hard way that I must minister from my encounter with Christ. And, not only that, but I also cannot minister from yesterday's encounter. I must continually be encountered by Christ and minister from this—from today's encounter.

Intimacy in Prayer

The word "intimacy" comes from the Latin word *intimus*, which means "inmost, innermost, deepest." It connotes a level of vulnerability, of "being exposed." In the account of the fall, we know Adam and Eve hid from this intimacy after they had sinned. Sin impacted their daily walk with God—a dedicated time of vulnerability and sharing. They hid. (As an aside, I think God's first question he issues to humanity as recounted in Genesis 3:9 is one of the most haunting in all the Bible: "Where are you?" When we sin, we step out of relationship and, in doing so, we lose ourselves, so to speak.)

Given our fallen and redeemed state, it is important to practice intimacy in prayer. It's a matter of vulnerability.

I've started referring to God as "Dad" in prayer. This sounds childish, though, really, it's childlike. If I call my earthly father "Dad," and in baptism, I've become an adopted son of God and Jesus refers to the Father as Abba (literally Dad or Daddy), then why not call God "Dad"? This is an entry into the life of the Holy Spirit, for "God sent the spirit of his Son into our hearts, crying out, 'Abba, Father!'" (Gal 4:6). It means entering the Son's intimate way of praying to his Abba (who is our Abba, too). It means praying with the trust and obedience of a beloved child.

This simple shift in diction breaks down barriers and opens my prayer to a new level of vulnerability—a deeper intimacy. If you're "stuck" in your life of prayer or feeling like God is distant, you might consider these simple prompts:

- "Dad, you are _____" (fill in the blank with some expressions of praise like "awesome, almighty King of kings, Lord of lords," etc.).

- "Thank you for _____" (fill in this blank by naming ways in which your Dad has blessed you since your last appointment with him).

- "Dad, I am _____" (let God know how you're doing and what's going on. Be as vulnerable as possible. This is where you bring your loneliness to bear with all its "weight").

- "Dad, I need _____" (let God know what you need from him and intercede for others who need his providential action in their lives).

Committing to Prayer

To live from the inside out means prioritizing prayer. It means making the interior life your number one thing. Rather than carrying out the heresy of good works, Jesus calls us to abide in him, to "be with him," to sit at his feet like Mary—in an enduring posture of prayer.

Most ministers don't pray because they've substituted work for prayer. This has been the case for me in ministry from time to time. I'd get busy with ministry, and ministry bled into everything—including my prayer time. Eventually, I stopped speaking with and listening to God, and that time I used to spend in prayer became devoted to merely thinking about God or thinking about ministry. I no longer had time for God. I was too busy working for him to talk to him. In those times, it became clear that my priorities were out of whack. For most people, not praying is not so much an I-don't-have-time thing as it is a priority thing. That has been the case for me, and still is, from time to time. We find time for what we prioritize. Not prioritizing prayer is a bad reason to not pray. Fortunately, there's a simple way to get back on track with prayer.

If you look at your calendar, you will see what your priorities are—they take up blocks of time during your day. You write your priorities on your calendar or add them into your calendar app. We put appointments in calendars and we don't want to miss them—we won't miss them—because they're priorities.

Building on this basic premise, Fr. Michael Scanlan invites us to reconsider our priorities by making an appointment with God. "What does it mean to have an appointment?" he asks. "It means you make some kind of commitment to be somewhere at such and such an hour, at such and such a place to meet with so and so."[15] Not surprisingly, these are the key elements of making a prayer appointment with God. You know when you will meet, where you will meet, and with whom you will meet.

If God, and abiding relationship with him, is your top priority, then prayer should appear on your calendar. After reading Fr. Scanlan's book, this is exactly what I did. My prayer time, my appointment with God, now appears on my calendar. I have to carve out that time and space or it simply won't happen. It has to be a priority and I can't be trying to do anything else during that time. It doesn't need to be super long, but it does need to be super focused. The *Catechism* talks about the importance of setting aside time for praying with a singular focus:

> Prayer is the life of the new heart. It ought to animate us at every moment. But we tend to forget him who is our life and our all. This is why the Fathers of the spiritual life . . . insist that prayer is a remembrance of God often awakened by the memory of the heart: "We must remember God more often than we draw breath." But *we cannot pray "at all times" if we do not pray at specific times*, consciously willing it. (CCC §2697)

It is true, St. Paul tells us to "pray without ceasing" (1 Thess 5:17). Pray "at all times," he says. But, we can't pray always if we don't pray at specific times. I call these "prayer anchors." You need

15. Scanlan, *Appointment with God*, 15.

certain fixed points that the thread of prayer hangs upon throughout the day.

Again, when making an appointment/scheduling a meeting, you know who the appointment is with, when, where, and for approximately how long the appointment will last. You also typically know the content of the appointment—what you will be discussing, etc. Let's apply this to prayer:

- With whom? (I'll give you the answer to this one: *God*.)

- When will you meet? If God is most important, he should get the best time of day. In general, what is the best time for you to pray?[16] (Be very specific.)

- Where will you meet? (Setting) What is a solitary place where you won't be too distracted? Where will you pray each day?

- How long will you meet? Consider making a commitment that will bend, but not break you. What is a reasonable time commitment? (Consider at least ten minutes at a minimum. Though, we should keep in mind what St. Francis de Sales once said: "Every one of us needs half an hour of prayer a day, except when we are busy—then we need an hour.")

It is worth noting that the appointment with God should be shrouded in silence. As Robert Cardinal Sarah puts it in *The Power of Silence*, "At the heart of man there is an innate silence, for God abides in the innermost part of every person. God is silence, and this divine silence dwells in man."[17] We hear God speak to us in silence. For this appointment, we should cultivate exterior silence

---

16. Fr. Scanlan points out that Jesus frequently rose early and went off to pray. Following Jesus' lead, Scanlan believes praying right away in the morning is best. I agree. I've made this my practice. Generally, my appointment with God takes place right away and it happens while sipping my coffee. As Ven. Fulton Sheen once said: "The average American is physically, biologically, physiologically and neurologically unable to do anything worthwhile before he has a cup of coffee! And that goes for prayer too . . . Let them have coffee before meditation."

17. Sarah, *Power of Silence*, 22.

(e.g., praying before the kids wake up, with cell phone off, etc.), because interior silence is well worth it.

Your Prayer Time Is *Your* Prayer Time

Exactly what your prayer time looks like, exactly what your appointment with God, your conversation with God looks like, will vary from person to person.

I think some people become overwhelmed at the thought of praying because the Catholic Church, in her commitment to God and over the course of her 2000 years, has developed quite an array of devotions. Admittedly, it can be overwhelming. Should I pray the Rosary or the Chaplet? Should I petition God or sit in silence? Do I use my own words or a traditional prayer? Some people become paralyzed in prayer the same way you become paralyzed at the grocery store when presented with too many options in the cereal aisle.

The bottom line is this: The right way to pray for you is the right way to pray for you.

As I recall the last twenty years of my life, I see a relatively stable commitment to prayer and I see that my prayer has taken on many forms. There are times and seasons in prayer. At one time, a particular devotion surfaces and bears fruit. At other times, a different devotion may do the same. Regardless of these devotions, I can point to two elements or ingredients that have remained consistent fixtures in my daily appointment with God throughout this time: (1) lectio divina and (2) daily Mass. I would like to tease these out a bit.

Lectio Divina

Lectio divina (i.e., divine or holy reading) is a method of meditating on Scripture such that one hears a personal word (or words) from the Lord. God's words in Scripture are "living and effective" (Heb 4:12), and in these words God speaks to us. Lectio, then, is not about sophisticated Bible study or deep exegesis, valuable as these might be. Instead, lectio is more about taking up the posture of a child who listens for the voice of his or her Father. In lectio, God reaches us as a loving Father who wants to speak a word of love into the lives of his children.

People often attribute lectio divina to St. Benedict of Nursia (sixth century). However, its true origins date back to the earliest monastic communities of Christianity. Regardless, the earliest monastic version of lectio brought together memorization and meditation. A monk would read the Scriptures, while listening for and following the movement of the Holy Spirit. It was unstructured, in a sense, methodless. It really was a kind of ruminating on the word by reading, reflecting, responding, and resting.

For these early monastic communities, lectio had a threefold goal which endures to this day: (1) to draw close to God's word; (2) to assimilate it into the whole of one's life; and (3) to better hear the word of God throughout the rest of the day.[18] Said another way, by drawing close to God's word and "ingesting it," so to speak, it becomes part of you. And, by learning how to hear God's voice in Scripture, we can hear the echoes of God's voice throughout the day.

A later form, which might be called medieval, because it developed in the twelfth century, presents us with more distinctive steps. It's a more clearly defined method. This comes to us from a Carthusian prior named Guigo II. He characterized lectio as a ladder with four distinguished stages or rungs: Reading, Meditation, Prayer, and Contemplation. There's a basic movement in terms of who is doing most of the acting. On the lower rungs, I am engaging in vocal prayer (I'm reading, thinking, meditating, praying, speaking), and it gives way to listening, to contemplation—where God is the principal actor. In contemplation, I am more passive. I am receiving. As Trappist monk Charles Cummings puts it, "Reading and meditation are accomplished by my grace-assisted, natural powers; in prayer I am partly active, partly acted upon by God; on

---

18. See Cummings, *Monastic Practices*, 8–9.

the highest rung, contemplation, the word of God grips and draws me, carrying me into itself."[19]

Recently, Pope Benedict XVI encouraged the practice of lectio divina as a source of spiritual nourishment for every believer. He went on to describe each of the steps of this ancient prayer method. I have compiled the basic steps of lectio divina as Benedict XVI lays them out:[20]

1. *Opening Prayer*: Open with a prayer to the Holy Spirit, asking for the grace to hear the word of God deeply, and to respond to the word personally.

2. *Reading (*lectio*)*: Read the passage a first time—slowly. Allow the word to "wash over you," so to speak. Simply grasp the basics of what the passage is saying as a whole. We read with, as Pope Benedict XVI says, "a desire to understand its true content: what does the biblical text say in itself? Without this, there is always a risk that the text will become a pretext for never moving beyond our own ideas." What is this text about? Who are the characters? What are the circumstances? What teaching is being presented?

3. *Meditation* (meditatio): Read the passage a second time. "*What does the biblical text say to us?* Here, each person," Benedict XVI says, "must let himself or herself be moved and challenged." What word or phrase stands out to you? Write that down. What does this word/phrase mean in light of the passage as a whole? Ponder. Consider. Take time to wrestle with the words, and to meditate on them in silence.

4. *Prayer* (oratio): "Following this comes prayer (*oratio*), which asks the question: *what do we say to the Lord in response to his word?*" Talk to God. Speak with him. What do you say to God in response to the word(s) spoken to you? Ask him what he's trying to say: Father, why are you speaking these words? Have

19. Cummings, *Monastic Practices*, 8–9.

20. Please note that all direct quotations in this lectio guide can be found in Benedict XVI, *Verbum Domini*, §87.

a loving conversation. Repent. Adore. Beg. Intercede. Express gratitude. Listen.

5. *Contemplation* (contemplatio): "Finally, lectio divina concludes with contemplation (*contemplatio*), during which we take up, as a gift from God, his own way of seeing and judging reality, and ask ourselves *what conversion of mind, heart and life is the Lord asking of us?*" Contemplation is pure gift. On our part, it is pure receptivity. If the mind is active in steps 1–4, here, the mind rests, is passive, and receives. Try to rest in the word in silence. Listen. What is God saying? How is he inviting conversion?

6. Closing Prayer: Conclude by praying the Our Father.

7. *Action* (actio): Pope Benedict XVI says, "We do well also to remember that the process of *lectio divina* is not concluded until it arrives at action (*actio*), which moves the believer to make his or her life a gift for others in charity." Lectio should *bear fruit* in the action, the stuff of our lives. Pay attention to how the seed of the word bears fruit in your life. Keep a journal as a testimony of transformation.

Please note: The stages of lectio divina are not air-tight steps. In other words, the steps are not fixed, but are more like guidelines for how the prayer normally proceeds. It should be a natural movement toward greater simplicity with less talking and more listening. One must be open to the Holy Spirit.

Daily Mass

I've admittedly waffled in my commitment to daily Mass over the years. As an undergrad at Franciscan University, I attended Mass nearly every day of the week. Early in my time of youth ministry, I guess I thought I was too busy to spend the thirty minutes in Mass, or that the 100 feet I had to walk from my office in the parish center to the church was too far. The misprioritization is embarrassing now that I think about it.

Getting to Mass is the other part of my daily appointment with God. One flows into the other. I read the daily Mass readings and pray lectio with the daily Gospel, then, a few hours later, I attend holy Mass—feeding on the words of Scripture yet again and receiving the Word sacramentally in the Eucharist.

When we participate in holy Mass, we are participating in the Church's highest form of prayer. Pope Benedict XVI says this:

> The Eucharistic Celebration is the greatest and highest act of prayer, and constitutes the centre and the source from which even the other forms receive "nourishment": the Liturgy of the Hours, Eucharistic adoration, Lectio divina, the Holy Rosary, meditation.[21]

It's the highest form of prayer because it is not just humans praying, but God himself interceding for us. During the Mass, Christ's sacrifice on the cross is truly re-presented on the altar (cf. CCC §1366). We sacramentally celebrate the Son's perfect offering to the Father on our behalf, and we join in his offering by uniting our prayers to his.

I've come to appreciate the ritual nature of the Mass over the years. The rituals are like a rushing river. You simply have to get into the stream and the current, the ritual, takes you from there. You have to try hard to not be moved. When all other ways of prayer seem to fail or not bear fruit, when I feel like I'm working so hard and not making any progress, when I am distracted as all get-out and show up to Mass with my head in a thousand other places, I can just allow the Mass to be what it is and move me. Taking this a step further, the ritual of the Mass is not only a synchronic occurrence. It's not only jumping into *this* sacred river for thirty or sixty minutes. No, you come to realize that this river has been flowing for nearly 2,000 years, with the same basic ritual structure carrying people to the Father, through the Son, and in the Holy Spirit. It's overwhelming when you think about it.

I know plenty of people who become frustrated with themselves for being distracted at Mass and failing to enter in. I'm one

---

21. Benedict XVI, "Homily—May 3, 2009."

of these people. Once, I was expressing my frustration to a former teen of mine (who is now a seminarian). He could empathize. He said that he thinks about it like the thousands of meals he's eaten in his lifetime. He needed to eat all those meals to be nourished and grow. Most of these meals are not memorable, but they are necessary. However, in their ordinariness, they are forgettable.

Acknowledging the limitations of this analogy, he said the Mass is similar. Every Mass is necessary for our spiritual growth. Every time we participate in the eucharistic meal, we grow and are transformed, even if we forget the particulars of this or that Mass, or fail to be attentive throughout the whole of a given Mass. Of course, we all have *those Masses* that we'll never forget. Those instances where, for whatever reason, we were open to receive God's grace and were attentive to it in an unforgettable way. But, even when this doesn't happen, the Mass is still effective in nourishing us for the mission of our lives.

A Waste of Time

Learning to live from the inside out, starting with that innermost point of the interior life, the relationship with God, means learning to waste time with God. Lovers waste time together. They spend time together, sometimes huge amounts of time, for no purpose other than being with each other. They will go to great lengths, overcome tremendous distances, for time together. They are prodigals with their time, lavishly wasting it on each other for no pragmatic gain. True lovers are not utilitarians.

Unfortunately, we live in a utilitarian world dominated by feasibility studies, data analysis, and outcomes assessments. We're trained to consider it wasteful to spend time and energy on something that offers no practical, worldly gain. Yet lovers must spend time and energy wastefully for love to grow. Prayer and liturgy is how love with God grows. For all intents and purposes, in the eyes of the world, it's a complete waste of time. This is also exactly why it's the most valuable of all time—in fact, it's so important that it orders the rest of our time.

Romano Guardini expresses this need to spend time with God powerfully, when he likens it to a form of "play," saying:

> The soul must learn to abandon, at least in prayer, the restlessness of purposeful activity; it must learn to waste time for the sake of God, and to be prepared for the sacred game with sayings and thoughts and gestures, without always immediately asking "why?" and "wherefore?" It must learn not to be continually yearning to do something, to attack something, to accomplish something useful, but to play the divinely ordained game of the liturgy in liberty and beauty and holy joy before God.[22]

In the daily appointment with God, which for me consists of lectio divina and holy Mass, I abide in my baptismal identity by wasting time with God. It's easily the best time of the day, even if it's the most unproductive in the eyes of the world.

Conclusion

Following this treatment of the interior life, I will move into chapters on primary vocation and Catholic ministry. If it seems as though our interior lives can sometimes be in shambles, family life and parish life present a host of difficulties. Every family struggles with its own forms of dysfunction (largely due to the reality of sin). A parish is a dysfunctional family of dysfunctional families. What can allow us to remain at peace amid such dysfunction? The interior life.

Here, I'm reminded of the calming of the storm at sea in Matt 8:23–27:

---

22. Guardini, *Spirit of the Liturgy*, 40.

As Jesus got into a boat, his disciples followed him.
Suddenly a violent storm came up on the sea,
so that the boat was being swamped by waves;
but he was asleep.
They came and woke him, saying,
"Lord, save us! We are perishing!"
He said to them, "Why are you terrified, O you of little faith?"
Then he got up, rebuked the winds and the sea,
and there was great calm.
The men were amazed and said, "What sort of man is this,
whom even the winds and the sea obey?"

I've always found it curious that Jesus calls out the disciples for having little faith. Wasn't it an act of faith to wake Jesus up to save them? What is Jesus getting at? I think the answer to this has to do with the fact that Jesus was sleeping through the whole thing. What would allow him to rest amid such chaos? How could he be peaceful as the tempest raged? The answer has to be the love of the Father. He was always resting in, always abiding in, the love of the Father. This is what it means to have faith. Yes, there will be storms. Yes, there is dysfunction. But the love of the Father transcends all of it. And the practice of the interior life is precisely how we access that love within it.

—— 3 ——

Primary Vocation

She felt as though she had to sacrifice our relationship for the sake of the Church. She felt that if, in her frustration, she frustrated me and my (packed) ministry schedule, she would be actively opposing God. Therefore, to please God, she had to sacrifice her marriage. To love the Church, she had to sacrifice her husband.

These are some of the real sentiments my wife shared with me as we tried to navigate ministry together during the first chunk of our married life.

I had taken on a missionary mindset and was wholly given to the work. I rarely said "no" to anything asked of me or to any opportunity presented to me. My youth ministry bled into other parish ministries. My ministry at the parish bled into broader collaborative and diocesan ventures. I worked most nights and every Sunday. Quite often, I would be gone for a retreat, a conference, or a mission trip. It was all consuming. Oh, and I was working on a master's degree in theology. My wife and kids, if they got anything, got the scraps. They got whatever pittance of energy I had left.

Early in our marriage, I would justify my unorthodox work schedule (i.e., gobs of nights and weekends) to my wife. She would listen and nod with a kind of saddened expression on her face. After some years, I realized the look had changed. There was a fire of resentment in her eyes. She would make a pointed comment here or there. Occasionally, things would reach a boiling point. It was becoming clear that being wholly given to the ministry was driving a serious wedge between us. I became avoidant. The constant threat of conflict between us made the whole situation feel like walking on eggshells. If I recall correctly, we were then about five years into ministry, and five years into marriage.

To make matters worse, I was leading a dual life. I ministered to others, but not to my own. It occurred to me after a night of ministry that I can lead over a hundred teens in prayer, I can teach them about God, and so forth, but I never do these things at home. With my family, I was lethargic. Maybe it had to do with spending all my energy and brainpower on ministry at the church. But, more than that, I think it had to do with seeing few examples of a husband/father leading a Catholic family. I, quite honestly, had no idea what to do, so it was easiest to do nothing. My family, raising my children, intimidated me. I could feel my insecurities all the time. So, I avoided it. Having gone to Franciscan University of Steubenville, I had seen people lead ministry. I learned what to do by watching it and participating in it for several years. Catholic family life, though, felt foreign.

Clearly, my life was off balance. Significantly so. Considering Jim Beckman's inside out model, it's not even necessarily that I was living from the outside in all the time. I was praying through most of these early years—at least more often than not. It was more like that the middle circle—vocation—didn't exist. I would simply leapfrog right over it, from prayer to ministry, and ministry to prayer.

Murphin Ridge

To this day, I cannot remember exactly why we decided to do this, but six years into our marriage we lined up a babysitter (probably my in-laws) and headed to Murphin Ridge Inn. Murphin Ridge is a bed and breakfast about an hour or so east of Cincinnati. It's in the foothills of the Appalachians. There, removed from the intensity of our ministry and family life, my wife shared the depths of her hurt with me. She revealed how lonely she had been and how she felt abandoned by me and by God. She let me know how she felt she had to sacrifice our relationship in order to appease God—that this was somehow her calling in life.

I was shocked.

As noted above, I wasn't completely oblivious. I had been picking up on her body language and sensed the hurt in her eyes in the months leading up to this. I wasn't surprised she was hurting, but the level of spiritual desolation rocked me. It was like Genesis 3 was being rerun in our marriage. The enemy was sowing seeds of doubt, assaulting her with lies, and I was just sitting there letting it happen—or simply leaving the garden of our marriage to go tend the other spiritual gardens I'd been entrusted with in ministry. I cared more about saving other souls than those of my own family. I cared more about helping others than helping my wife.

As all this surfaced, I knew I had to act. I apologized. I made some immediate schedule changes and imposed new boundaries to attempt some sort of division between ministry and life (which, I realize, is a rather gray space). We decided to stop hosting some ministry gatherings in our home to carve out more time devoted to our family. These were small but necessary steps, and it kicked off a process of healing and reprioritizing that continues to this day.

Reprioritizing

After our retreat to Murphin Ridge, our process of learning how to navigate ministry and marriage was not suddenly smooth. There were still some dark valleys and some tall peaks. Over time, though, we have gotten things to smooth out and seem to have struck a decent balance. I would like to walk through a few of the significant moments along the way, as they might provide insight and inspiration for others trying to hold together marriage and ministry. As I think about it, this process consisted of two complementary parts. The first was largely interior and personal, while the second involved actively strengthening my marriage and family life.

Interior Shifts

Following Murphin Ridge, a series of spiritual shifts took place as living from the inside out took hold and my interior life flowed into my primary vocation rather than around it.

Applying the Fruits of Lectio to Family

For many years, as I would pray lectio divina each morning, I would search for inspiration for ministry. How do these words speak into my ministry? What's God's will for the people of the parish? This was constantly on my mind and because if God wanted me to bear apostolic fruit, it made sense that he would announce his will and inspire me. Consequently, my time of lectio devolved into a lot of "think-praying." This means I was thinking about praying and substituting thinking for praying. In the end, I was working.

The first real interior shift for living from the inside out came when I simply *let the Lord speak to me.* Lectio is primarily about God speaking to me before it's about God speaking through me to anyone else. This took a lot of pressure off my prayer time, as I could simply *be with God* without pressure to get something out of it for others.

As this shift took hold, I found God speaking into my son-ship, to be sure, but I also began hearing him speak into my roles as husband and father. In other words, God was speaking into my fundamental identities and bringing about the overflow from my interior life to my primary vocation. The inside out thing wasn't some herculean effort I had to carry out on my own. Instead, God desired for me to live from the inside out, and he brought it about. I simply had to stop treating my prayer time as work—as an idea session with God for my ministry—and open to God's word as his beloved son.

Intercessory Prayer

I find a poem by Robert Hayden striking. It's called "Those Winter Sundays."[1] Hayden describes how, even on Sundays, his father rose early and got dressed in the "blueblack cold." With hands aching from a long week of work, he made a fire. The boy Hayden says, "I'd wake and hear the cold splintering, breaking. / When the rooms were warm, he'd call, / and slowly I would rise and dress." His father would warm the house, then rouse the children. There's something beautifully intimate about this image of family life. You get a sense of the dignified role of the father as a provider and a protector.

In the early years of ministry, I'd rise early and add to the blueblack cold of my house by cracking open the laptop, blue light streaming out as I slaved over the keyboard, working. As the interior shift took hold, however, my actions changed. This holds true today. First things first. I make my coffee and I pray. I see my prayer as something of a fire, burning not only for my own spiritual warmth, but for that of my family as well. This prayer, though weary, warms me and the house also. I find this to be especially true in my intercessory prayer for my family. Somehow, these prayers of a father—prayed alone, sitting on the couch—break the blueblack cold that seeps into family life and allow the warmth of the Holy Spirit to come into our home.

Be the Father

In the Introduction of Henri Nouwen's *The Return of the Prodigal Son,* the Dutch priest recounts that he often identified with one of the two sons in the parable of the lost son (Luke 15:11–32). However, when he moved into the L'Arche community in Toronto, a woman in the community explained to him that whether Nouwen was the older son in the parable of the lost son, or the younger one, "you are called to become the father." Nouwen much preferred to be one of the sons, and had never thought of himself as the father. She continues:

1. Hayden, "Those Winter Sundays," 41.

You have been looking for friends all your life; you have been craving for affection as long as I've known you; you have been interested in thousands of things; you have been begging for attention, appreciation, and affirmation left and right. The time has come to claim your true vocation—to be a father who can welcome his children home . . . We need you to be a father who can claim for himself the authority of true compassion.[2]

Nouwen was in his mid-fifties at the time. He had long been a priest, a father figure in the Church, without embracing it. It is possible to be something without owning it. It is possible to be a husband or a father without embracing that identity and living accordingly. As I read Nouwen's Introduction, these words from his friend struck me like lightning. I did not want to wait until I was fifty or sixty to finally decide to be a father. My kids would all be grown and gone. I needed to embrace this now, with my whole heart. It had already been too long (about ten years into marriage).

My heart had not caught up with my head. I had understood the inside-out image and had taken some practical steps toward working it out. There had even been some interior shifts. But I had not yet made a deep, *interior decision for it*. I had not yet *willed to be a father* from the depths of my heart. My heart needed to catch up with my head (and with my life circumstances) and Nouwen's self-realization provoked my own.

Leaving Ministry (and Coming Back)

As this ongoing interior shift took place—the lectio, the praying for my family, the deeper embrace of my fatherly identity—I became more aware of an unhealthy ministry situation I found myself in. It was a combination of unreasonable expectations, way too many nights and weekends at the church, and an unhealthy staff situation. I could see, quite clearly, the toll it was taking on my family. And, with more kids and older kids, I could no longer shuffle off the pressure on my family by simply saying "the kids are young,

2. Nouwen, *Return of the Prodigal Son*, 22.

they won't remember." No. It was a crucial moment for our family. My oldest was in junior high and my wife was drowning at home. We couldn't keep up the crazy hours any longer. Praying with the Gospel of Matthew one morning, my time of lectio drove all this home with a personalized line: What profit would there be for one to gain all the souls in the world for Christ and forfeit *those of his family*? (cf. Matt 16:26).

After several months of trying to work things out at the parish, nothing changed. So, I left ministry for the sake of my family. I found a secular job with a great company and immediately felt relief at home. I had my nights and weekends back, and I had the energy I needed to invest in the relationships that mattered most. This was a necessary season in life. After months of getting myself and my family healthy again, I sensed the call to get back into ministry. And I responded. But from a different place. By this point, that living from the inside out had become a concrete reality. I re-entered ministry with clear priorities and well-established boundaries. I now work for a pastor who understands and supports my primary vocation, not just with words, but with concrete actions as well. In fact, in many ways, my ministry happens after and as an overflow of my ministry to my family as husband and father.

Leaving ministry was hard and shocking (for me and for many others). But, it was necessary at the time. Something serious had to change and my wife and kids needed to know, deeply, that they were more important than church work. They *are* more important than church work, so the hard decision became easy to make as months wore on with no change at the parish. As it turns out, that year away from ministry was probably one of the best ministry decisions I've ever made.

(By the way, I'm not the only person who's done something like this. I know several men my age who left ministry for a season, only to return to it a year or so down the road. One guy even took up a painting job for the year. He called it his "St. Joseph Year." I can appreciate that.)

Exterior Shifts

If the previous list catalogs changes that happened in me, I'd like to add to this list changes in my relationship with my wife and our children. Some of these shifts might seem rather pedestrian, but anyone who has tried to change well-entrenched patterns of living knows this is not the case.

Connect and Pray in the Morning

For many years, especially when the kids were young, I would leave the house in a hurry and be off to the races. I'd kiss Katie (my wife) goodbye and be at the church till who knows when. I might or might not call her or send her a text during the day. In other words, we didn't connect much before I left, and that disconnectedness remained throughout the day.

When I began working for the Archdiocese of Cincinnati, I suddenly had a commute. We got in the habit of talking on the phone while I drove into downtown Cincinnati, and we'd conclude our conversation with a Hail Mary and the St. Michael Prayer—invoking Mary's intercession for our family, as well as St. Michael's protection. This habit has stuck throughout the years to the point where my day seems "off" if we don't connect over the phone. (For those of you who are wondering why we have to connect over the phone instead of in person, we have eight children, so we usually spend the morning tripping over each other to get the kids out the door and to the bus stop.)

With my new position as a director of evangelization for four parishes, I'm often traveling between locations during the day. This gives me another opportunity to check in with my wife. I find these conversations throughout the day, however brief, incredibly helpful for our relationship. We are more connected. We are on the same page.

This simple practice of making the phone call reminds me of attachment theory. Twentieth-century psychologists John Bowlby and Mary Ainsworth developed it. In a nutshell, attachment theory holds that human life is deeply relational. The most foundational relationships (that of a child and parents or primary caregivers) radically shape the way we engage with reality. Persons are made to live confidently and securely because of the relationship with the attachment figure (e.g., mother, father, etc.), who acts as both a safe haven and a secure base. As a safe haven, the attachment figure provides safety and surety in the midst of a distressing situation. The child runs to the safe haven.

But the attachment figure also acts as a base of security, providing the relational stability that makes it possible for the child to venture out into the world for exploration and ultimately to make a unique contribution. When a child lacks such attachment figures, when insecurely attached, life unravels.[3] As we grow older, our attachment figures may change. Adults do not run home to Mom and Dad every time they face fear or frustration, but spouses may (and should!) turn to each other. Marriage provides each spouse with a new attachment figure (see Gen 2:24). Connecting in the morning, and even during the day, when possible, builds stronger attachment between my wife and me.

Weekly Date Night

As life takes off with ministry and children, it's easy for spouses to become pseudo-business partners or co-project managers. It's as if you're running a small enterprise and the day-to-day affairs take precedence over any relational depth. A weekly date night can be an antidote to banality. Earlier in our marriage, we could not afford to pay for a babysitter and go out every week (still can't), but we could do something like this once a month or so. We relished those moments to get out of the house and enjoy a meal and an uninterrupted conversation. On date nights spent at home, we'd feed the kids early and get them to bed or put on a movie, then we'd fix dinner for ourselves and eat alone. Occasionally we'd watch a movie together or recite poetry. Now, often, we simply have a

---

3. See McLeod, "Attachment Theory in Psychology."

45

meal together and try to have a deeper conversation than usual. I've found over the years that the content or snazziness of the date doesn't matter as much as its occurrence.

Annual Retreat

Ever since we went to Murphin Ridge, we've made it a point to have an annual retreat. This is not fancy. It's usually a two-day, one-night sort of thing. But, it gives us an opportunity to review the past year, talk through our relationship with each kid, look ahead to the next year and adjustments we need to make, and (most importantly) to dream a bit about the life we're building together. I suppose we're usually too idealistic and follow-through wanes on some of the resolutions we make, but that's life. The annual retreat allows us to hear the voice of God and to respond. When we get back home to the eight kids, that's when the rubber meets the road. At least there's some air back in our relational tires.

Saying "Yes" to Ministry

I remember being quite a few years into parish ministry and suddenly feeling trapped. I had a master's in theology and a bunch of years of youth ministry experience under my belt. It seemed like I'd boxed myself into a career corner and there was no way out. Just "keep doing ministry" was my default position. Naturally, this means it was my wife's, too. We were kind of slogging it out, raked over the coals of one intense ministry year after another. At least we were more on the same page in our relationship and regarding ministry, but we still felt like slaves to our circumstances, slaves to the Church.

Around this time, I had a conversation with a friend in ministry. He said he and his wife had this exact same feeling and realized that they were now choosing ministry as a positive choice for their life. In other words, instead of simply defaulting to another year of ministry and being frustrated by the cost to their family life, they were looking at what another year of ministry would cost their marriage and family life, and they were choosing it as a positive value. They would say "yes" to another year—committing to one year at a time. This seemed to be spot on to us, so we started making it an annual practice each spring. We would take some time to consider how the last year went and what another year of ministry would mean for our family. Following this time of personal discernment and numerous conversations, we could, in greater freedom, choose to commit to another year of ministry after fully counting the cost. In other words, we went from taking a negative position towards ministry, as if we were saying: "I guess we can't leave and do something else," to "yes, we're in!" This is not only a healthier approach to ministry, it's healthier for marriage as well.

Annual Calendaring

Early in ministry, the ministry calendar dictated our life. I would plan it and inform Katie about it. Then, during the year, new opportunities would arise. I'd commit to those and inform Katie about them. I was constantly springing new commitments on her. "I'll actually be gone tomorrow night," or "Next Saturday morning, I now have a meeting." These lines often came from my lips. It was like we could exercise no dominion over our life. Ministry took priority and our family had to submit.

Around the same time as we started saying "yes" to ministry and committing for a year, we shifted how we calendared. Instead of calendaring ministry events first, we calendared our family first. What did our family need? We mapped our vacation, days off, and so forth. I also started to establish a defined day off each week. Initially, I had no dedicated day off. It would simply shift from week to week based on the needs of ministry, and sometimes it wouldn't happen at all. It was not uncommon for me to go a few weeks at a time without a real day off. As our family grew, I eventually started taking two days off each week (like a normal person's weekend), though this usually consisted of taking Friday and Saturday for the family, as Sunday was a workday.

47

Calendaring together got us on the same page, and we could see that our family's life and time was first. Then, ministry had to fit into *our* schedule and not the other way around. Obviously, some concessions had to be made and there were times things that had to be finessed. This is still the case. And obviously, new ministry opportunities arose during the year that require discernment and discussion. Again, still the case. But at least we have an established baseline for prioritizing family time rather than simply getting jockeyed by ministry demands week in and week out.

Weekly Catechesis

A few years ago, I had a conversation with a holy monsignor, a true octogenarian. I was bemoaning the difficulty of raising Catholic kids these days. Really, there was something deeper at play. Over the years, I'd been finding it easier to minister to parishioners and strangers than to my own family. It's like when I was home, I was "off duty" and disengaged. The good priest gave me some simple advice that got me started down a path that previously felt overwhelming:

> Pray with your kids. Pray the Rosary and you will be okay. And teach them. My mother learned the faith from her father. Every Sunday, he would open the Bible and reach and teach the family. This is how my mother learned the faith. It was simple. Her father read the Bible and taught them from his experience.

This insight was the spark. If I could lead people to Christ in ministry, I could lead my family. And, if I was going to try to educate my children in the truth, I had to *do something*. Good intentions could only go so far. So the good monsignor's model was simple enough it gave me the confidence I needed to try. So, I talked to my wife, and we went for it.

For years now, we've had a brief (fifteen to thirty minutes depending on the number of questions the kids raise) time of "family catechesis" on Sundays. This has become a foundational moment in our house for talking about meaningful things in light of what God has to say about them. We let his word drive the conversation, initiate the conversation, and we respond to it. My wife and I open the floor for reflections and questions, and we share and respond. Over time, this moment of family catechesis has resulted in many important conversations about the culture and a Christian vision of reality. It allows us to name the truth about things and impart a Christian vision. We can then critique the culture with that vision, naming the parts of the culture that are good, true, and beautiful, and identifying the parts that are not. The Sunday family catechesis serves as the basis for numerous other conversations that take place throughout the week. It is something of a metronome of meaning—a steady teaching opportunity for me and my wife that remains in the background throughout the other days of the week. Do we always have all the answers? Nope. But we are present to the kids and take their questions seriously—and join in their quest for answers.

Wasting Time

Earlier in this book, I talked about wasting time with God. Wasting time with God is part of growing in the interior life. It's simply a necessary part of this growth. You need that quality time to fall in love with God. Well, you need quality time to fall in love with your family, too.

This is what the Sabbath is all about. Wasting time with God and wasting time together.

We work to rest. We work to have leisure.

This reminds me of *Field of Dreams*. In the movie, Ray Kinsella hears that mysterious voice telling him: "If you build it, he will come." This sets the whole plot in motion, as Ray razes precious acres of crop to build a baseball field on which the ghosts of the 1919 White Sox and other players with unrealized dreams can play baseball again. Ray's relentless efforts to "go the distance," to cultivate the land and avoid foreclosure on the property, ultimately results in an opportunity to ease his father's pain. Ray had a broken relationship that had never been reconciled before his father John's death. John, who had his own big-league dreams dissipate, appears on the field. Ray recognizes his father as a young man, and as John follows the rest of the old-timers off the diamond and toward the corn field, Ray utters that famous line: "Hey Dad . . . you wanna have a catch?" John accepts. Father and son are reconciled over a game of catch.

This scene strikes me. Perhaps because of my own memories of playing catch with my father. Perhaps because of tossing the ball with my own boys. But it also strikes me because the whole effort, all of Ray's consternation, leads to a game of catch. It literally leads to a waste of time. Playing catch is a waste of time. It serves no utilitarian purpose. It's pure leisure. By building, by working, Ray's father came. By going the distance, he could ease his father's pain by wasting time with him. In the final scene, the shot pans out and you see hundreds of cars snaking through the dirt roads of Iowa and heading towards the farm—those who would pay admission to watch the old-timers play on Ray's field and provide means of revenue necessary to keep the farm.

I see this as a tremendous image of family life. That we work together for the sake of wasting time together—to have that leisure wherein it seems like time stops.

Ministry cannot suffocate the time a family needs to waste together.

— 4 —

Ministry

This chapter catalogs several lessons I've learned while trying to minister more from a place of interiority, rather than relying on external techniques, strategies, and human devices. To live from the inside out, as one who ministers, means ministering from the inside out. One must allow that reservoir of the spiritual life to first water the fields of one's primary vocation before irrigating those of ministry. If you're ministering from the inside out, everything said in this chapter could be equally applied to marriage. Said another way, this chapter is the spiritual fruitfulness born from vocation. It is vocational fruitfulness applied to ministry. To throw another metaphor in the mix: I have in my mind an image of a cascading waterfall, a single stream of water originating from one Source.

What does inside out ministry look like concretely? How does ministry change when it occurs from the inside out? What follows is not a comprehensive listing, but a modest attempt to identify some markers illustrating the difference it makes.

Christocentricity: Always Beginning with Christ

Hans Urs von Balthasar was not one for mincing words.

The late Benedict XVI recalls a handwritten note from Balthasar regarding a paper the young theologian had submitted to Balthasar for review: "The triune God, Father, Son and Holy Spirit—do not presuppose him, but present him!"[1] Do not assume God and that people are living godly lives. In a post-Christian world, we can basically assume the opposite. In a sense, the need is a *kerygmatic* one, we need to begin from square one each time. We need to constantly reinforce an evangelical cornerstone.

In *Razing the Bastions*, Balthasar comments on the perpetual danger of not going back to Christ, even while staying in the Catholic intellectual tradition: "To honor the tradition does not excuse one from the obligation of beginning everything from the beginning each time, not with Augustine or Thomas or Newman, but with Christ."[2] This, it seems to me, is a particular challenge. As the tradition washes away in our wider culture, people discover this or that theologian or school of thought, and they hold on with all their might. When this happens, we risk creating an ersatz Jesus—some watered-down caricature, but not the real thing. When this happens, we make Jesus in our image and after our likeness.

However, "In the beginning was the Word, and the Word was with God, and the Word was God" (John 1:1).

Theology begins with and from the Word, the *Logos*, and from the fullness of the revelation of the *Logos*, the incarnate *Logos*, Jesus Christ. Ministry is the same. The Word is God's *Logos*, God's reason, God's understanding. To say we begin with the Word means ministry does not begin with subjective experience, the latest philosophical fads, recent ministry trends, or a favorite theology. It means we don't have the first word. Rather, we respond to the Word. Everything we do is response. Everything begins with Christ. The Word spoken to us—God's revelation—is the proper context, so to speak, for theology and ministry. This is the "given," the foundation for ministry, education, evangelization, and what have you. We need Jesus to make and remake us (and by extension, our ministries) in his image and after his likeness.

Twelve years ago, I was at lunch with about a dozen youth ministers (i.e., friends) and one of my ministry friends raised this

1. Benedict XVI, *Western Culture*, 164.
2. Balthasar, *Razing the Bastions*, 34.

question: What do teens need today? After several "genius" replies, the guy who launched the leading question stood up and slammed the table with his hand. Everyone jolted to attention. Everyone in the whole restaurant did, too. "Jesus!" he exclaimed. "Today's teens need Jesus." His answer was so simple and so right. It cut through all the chatter about this or that program, this or that event, this or that youth ministry technique or method. At the bottom of all of it, today's teens need Jesus—they need to be introduced to the living and breathing Jesus and into a relationship with him. Everyone to whom we minister needs this introduction to Jesus and to be guided into deeper relationship with him, so each one of them can live from the inside out.

Eucharist: Turning to Christ's Real Presence

The Eucharist is the core, the locus of our missionary discipleship. As its source and summit of apostolic activity, the Eucharist, and deeper entry into its celebration and mystery, must be central to any programs of formation we develop.[3] This emphasis also guards against the constant temptation to rely on our own devices and to idolize our work.

As I reflect on my experiences in ministry over the last fifteen years, hands down, the most breakthrough conversion experiences have happened in front of the Blessed Sacrament—in Mass and in adoration. Most of my ministry, if I'm honest, involves helping to bring people before Jesus in the Blessed Sacrament and he does the work. Jesus is *the* Evangelist. Eucharistic conversions make this clear.

Ratzinger articulates the reality:

> We might rather understand the Eucharist as being (if the term is correctly understood) the mystical heart of Christianity, in which God mysteriously comes forth, time and again, from within himself and draws us into his embrace . . . In order for mission to be more than propaganda for certain ideas or trying to win people

3. See Benedict XVI, *Sacramentum Caritatis*, art. 64.

over for a given community—in order for it to come from God and to lead to God, it must spring from a more profound source than that which gives rise to resource planning and the operational strategies that are shaped in that way. It must spring from a source both deeper and higher than advertising and persuasion. Is not the exhaustion of the missionary impulse in the last thirty years the result of our thinking only of external activities while having almost forgotten that all this activity must constantly be nourished from a deeper center? This center . . . is the Eucharist.[4]

Lectio: Giving God the First Word

It is easy to mindlessly move past the "obligatory" opening prayer and dive into the "guts" of any church-related meeting. There's a sense of needing to get to the real "stuff," so we sometimes mutter through the prayer and half-heartedly make the sign of the cross. This lackadaisical attitude is symptomatic of one that sees us as the real makers of things. We're the ones who are the movers and shakers. God is a formality—an ancillary reality. We're the ones to get the work done.

In the face of such a temptation, I appreciate the following message from Pope Benedict XVI:

> We cannot make the Church, we can only announce what he has done. The Church does not begin with our "making," but with the "making" and "speaking" of God. In the same way, the Apostles did not say, after a few meetings: now we want to make a Church, and that by means of a constituent assembly they were going to draft a constitution. No, they prayed and in prayer they waited, because they knew that only God himself can create his Church, that God is the first agent: if God does not act, our things are only ours and are insufficient; only God can testify that it is he who speaks and has spoken. Pentecost is the condition of the birth of the Church:

4. Ratzinger, *Pilgrim Fellowship of Faith*, 121–22.

only because God acted first, are the Apostles able to act with him and make what he does present. God has spoken and this "has spoken" is the perfection of faith but it is also always a present: the perfection of God is not only a past, because it is a true past that always carries in itself the present and the future. God has spoken means: "He speaks." And as at that time it was only on God's initiative that the Church could be born, that the Gospel could be known, the fact that God spoke and speaks, in the same way today only God can begin, we can only cooperate, but the beginning must come from God. So it is not a mere formality if we start our sessions each day with prayer: this corresponds to reality itself. Only God's precedence makes our journey possible, our cooperation, which is always cooperation, and not entirely our own decision. Therefore, it is important always to know that the first word, the true initiative, the true activity comes from God and only by inserting ourselves into the divine initiative, only by begging for this divine initiative, shall we too be able to become—with him and in him—evangelizers.[5]

If we are serious about always beginning with Christ and letting him have the first word, if we're serious about being able to give people Jesus, then in our meetings, in our planning, in our programs, we need to allow Jesus the first word. This needs to be concrete, or the first principles will be banished to the realm of pious idealism.

I once heard, through the Franciscan University alumni oral tradition, that when Fr. Michael Scanlan, TOR turned around Franciscan University of Steubenville, he established a culture of sharing in the word at the beginning of every meeting. I also heard that any time an important decision needed to be made, he went into eucharistic adoration and didn't leave until he knew from the Lord what should be done. I have never fact-checked this but based upon what I know of Franciscan University and Fr. Scanlan, it does not surprise me.

In my own ministry, I took up this sharing in the word as an essential starting point for most any meeting. Whatever team I've

5. Benedict XVI, "Meditation."

led, I decided to make lectio divina the common way in which we prayed our way into meetings and into decisions that needed to be made for the good of the ministry. In lectio divina, the Word speaks personally; but, as Benedict XVI notes, one must be attentive to an individualistic approach. "While it is a word addressed to each of us personally, it is also a word which builds community, which builds the Church."[6] Spending time working our way through the basic steps of lectio and not being afraid to share with one another the insights and movements that the word stirred within, not only helped us to grow in attentiveness to the word, but in attentiveness to, and trust in, each other. A community of leaders that learns how to hear the word of the Lord in Scripture and how it echoes through each other will learn to hear the word in ministry.

Role: Clarifying Lay Ministry from the Heart of the Church

Vatican II opened new pathways for lay people in the Church. Pope John Paul II describes the reality:

> The Church's mission of salvation in the world is realized not only by the ministers in virtue of the Sacrament of Orders but also by all the lay faithful; indeed, because of their Baptismal state and their specific vocation, in the measure proper to each person, the lay faithful participate in the priestly, prophetic and kingly mission of Christ.[7]

Regarding the laity, John Paul II is speaking of the "lay apostolate," which has to do with going forth or being sent out (that's what *apostolein* means in Greek). The words "lay apostolate" indicate an *ad extra* calling. Fr. James Mallon, in *Divine Renovation*, points out that after Vatican II, despite its emphasis on apostolate, "lay apostolate" became "lay ministry" and a certain kind of professional lay ministry emerged, along with its own form of clericalization.[8]

---

6. Benedict XVI, *Verbum Domini*, §86.

7. John Paul II, *Christifideles Laici*, §23.

8. Mallon, *Divine Renovation*, 78–79.

We can neither dismiss the call for lay apostolate, nor should we "clericalize" the laity.

This said, there is also a legitimate place for the lay person within the scope of pastoral ministry. John Paul II describes this in *Christifideles Laici*:

> When necessity and expediency in the Church require it, the Pastors, according to established norms from universal law, can entrust to the lay faithful certain offices and roles that are connected to their pastoral ministry but do not require the character of Orders.[9]

The pastor has a pastoral role—caring for the flock, feeding the flock, defending the flock. Fr. Mallon explains that overcoming the clericalization problem requires expanding the definition of pastoral ministry. Referencing Ephesians 4:11–13 and the call for various Church efforts to bring people to maturity, to full stature in Christ, Mallon claims "the end game of pastoral care is to bring people to maturity . . . to equip the saints for the work of ministry."[10] In other words, there is an *ad intra* need, and the pastor needs collaborators to help build up the Church. Lay people do need to be called into service.

But it doesn't stop with *ad intra* ministry. "Eventually, *ad intra* ministry reaches critical mass so that the desire to serve spills out into the community to become an apostolate," Mallon says.[11] Here, Mallon describes the move to *ad extra* apostolate, and a lay minister can play a critical role, as designated by the pastor, in shepherding this movement. The emphasis on the apostolate and equipping the laity for their role in it is the antidote to clericalism—clericalizing lay ministers.

All of this aligns with Canon Law's treatment of a parish. It says a parish "is to be territorial" (Can 515 §1); it is "a certain community of the Christian faithful stably constituted in a particular church, whose pastoral care is entrusted to a pastor" (Can 518). A

---

9. John Paul II, *Christifideles Laici*, §23.

10. Mallon, *Divine Renovation*, 82.

11. Mallon, *Divine Renovation*, 83.

parish is a geographical area, a region within which the pastor "is obliged to make provision so that the word of God is proclaimed in its entirety to those living in the parish . . . He is to make every effort, even with the collaboration of the Christian faithful, so that the message of the Gospel comes also to those who have ceased the practice of their religion or do not profess the true faith" (Can 528 §1). It is incumbent on the pastor, with the collaboration of the lay faithful, that the gospel be proclaimed within the whole of the parish.[12]

Obviously, this is a tremendous call: to shepherd the faithful to full stature and to bring the light of the gospel into all the dark places within a parish. In the face of such a task, the lay minister, as a key collaborator in the overall apostolate, needs to be given a clear understanding of the scope of his or her ministry from the pastor, along with a description of how it fits into the larger mission of the parish. The lay minister must know exactly what he or she has been given responsibility for and the degree to which he or she can make decisions for the sake of the parish apostolate. Such clarity guards against clericalization and burnout, and creates a healthy ministerial partnership between pastor and lay person. It allows one to minister from the inside, or the heart of the Church, under rightful authority.

Relationship: Getting Out of the Office

I remember telling my best ministry advice to a recent college graduate who was just hired by my parish to take over junior high youth ministry. I told her to get out of the office.

Too many ministers, it seems to me, spend entirely too much time at their desks. Admittedly, it's a safe place to be. Certain administrative things simply need to get done and engaging with lots of people distracts from this. I get it. But, if ministry is all about relationships, there's not much relationality going on when you're sitting by yourself in an office most of the week.

12. You can access the Catholic Church's *Code of Canon Law* at www.vatican.va/archive/cod-iuris-canonici/cic_index_en.html.

Early in my youth ministry experience, I realized that I was spending roughly 80 to 90 percent of my time each week in my office. I was working on flyers, writing talks, browsing the Internet for icebreaker ideas, and so forth. That left about 10 percent of my time for actually being with and ministering to teens.

That seemed crazy to me. As an introvert, I clearly needed to push myself to be more relational.

The first step out of this was a personal challenge. I decided that I was going to have at least two one-on-one meetings with teens at the local coffee shop each week. If I didn't have a conversation with at least two teens, then I would consider the week a failure.

Next, I layered in my Core Team members. I needed to have at least two one-on-ones with them. Then parents. And so forth.

Gradually, the proportion of time spent in my office vs. that spent building relationships shifted. The whole thing needed to be flipped on its head. How can I spend 80 percent of my time with the people to whom I am to minister? That became my question. I don't think I ever quite achieved that mark, but I do think it's a decent goal.

The bottom line is this: most of the time, the people to whom you minister are not in your office. Get out of your office and be with them. We must flip the proportion of time spent alone at the desk and that time spent building the relationships we've been tasked to build. Solid relationships of trust are central to thriving in ministry.

Hustle: Getting at the Secret Ingredient

Having worked at a Dominican parish for a number of years, I was blessed to become acquainted with St. Dominic's life. One story from his life has always struck me. Blessed Jordan of Saxony recounts it in the *Chronicle of the Origin of this Order*:

> Whilst he thus labored to make his own soul pleasing to God, the fire of divine love was daily more and more enkindled in his breast, and he was consumed with an ardent zeal for the salvation of infidels and sinners. To

> move the divine mercy to regard them with pity, he spent
> often whole nights in the church at prayer, watering the
> steps of the altar with abundance of tears, in which he
> was heard to sigh and groan before the Father of mercy,
> in the earnestness and deep affliction of his heart; never
> ceasing to beg with the greatest ardor, the grace to gain
> some of those unhappy souls to Christ.[13]

Whole nights in the church weeping for souls—pining for them to know God's love. It's an image that should move anyone engaged in parish ministry. Really, it's an image that should move any baptized person, for all are called to share in this mission.

For years now, I've been trying to help form the next generation of parish and youth ministers. It's hard. For some reason, it differs from programming robots—not that I've ever done that.

Once, I was talking to a longtime friend of mine who has also been doing full-time ministry. She said something quite interesting. She said she used to think she could just train and teach and raise up youth ministers like her (she was the diocesan youth director at the time of this conversation). But she was realizing it didn't work that way. She was kind of surprised to admit that the *person* of the youth minister had a lot more to do with it than she thought. It's not unlike what we know about teachers in schools. A person can go to university to become an educator, have all the requisite degrees and licenses, and still be a rather lousy teacher. Education and credentials, even experience, don't necessarily make for a good teacher. There's an intangible "teacherness" that someone either has or doesn't. I suppose ministry is the same and she picked up on this.

She went on to describe the "ministerness." "I think part of it is a matter of hustle," she observed. "Some people are willing to hustle for souls and most aren't." In other words, this isn't just "some job." It's not just pushing papers or advancing a career (as we understand this sort of thing today). It's not sitting at a desk for most of the week doing admin work or prepping a youth night. It's about relational hustle—the text messages, the prompt responses

13. Cited in Verner, "Tears of St. Dominic."

to email, the coffee meetings—and honing a craft with hard work. It's something of St. Dominic's zeal for souls. It's a lowercase "v" vocation and the people who have that knack for ministry and who get after it are the ones who seem to have the most fruitful ministries (which is not always a matter of numbers).

With an inside out approach, relational hustle flows from that striving for holiness, that constant pursuit of God (and allowing yourself to be pursued by him), followed by a vigorous living out of the relationships within your primary vocation. Ministerial hustle mirrors these more foundational hustles. All this said, hustle does not mean hurry. It has to do with a willingness to get after it and to put yourself out there.

Pace: On Slowing Down

Church buildings without air conditioning intrigue me. Inside of them, one is subject to the natural forces that determine the weather, and one feels his or her creatureliness. The people who built such churches were smart—employing cool stone throughout, and a series of stained-glass windows with long chains attached. The chains drape all the way down to hooks at about eye level for an adult. Typically, one is so captivated by the images in glass that the chains are unnoticeable, even though they are everywhere. This is all part of a system of what we might call natural climate control. One can do something to impact the atmospheric conditions (i.e., open or close some windows), but, overall, it is what it is. Again, one is subject to it.

Late one afternoon, it might have been in autumn, I was praying by myself in one such church. The windows were open and I could feel the cross-breeze. It was getting cooler outside. Consequently, it was getting cooler inside. A sacristan, aware of the dropping temperature, suddenly appeared. Taking note of me, the sole soul in the space attempting to pray, the sacristan quietly and with utmost reverence for the space (and my activity therein) closed specific windows. The man had to exercise great control over chains attached to windows five, ten, and even twenty feet above his head. The windows have a "catch" that holds them in an open position. One must pull the chain to release the window from the catch. Without care, restraint, and the exertion of muscle, the windows will then slam shut with great authority and considerable noise. Well, this sacristan quietly made his way about the church closing just the right windows and with ease. He moved carefully. He moved slowly. I did not hear a sound.

I was still distracted by him, but not because he was distracting. I was distracted because he was *not* distracting. I was distracted because I sensed the care with which he cared for the space and for me within it. He cared about my prayer. He cared about my soul.

As I returned to prayer, I became aware of the lesson. If this man closed windows with such care and concern for the individual soul, how much more should I exercise due concern for each person in my ministry?

So often I rush around in ministry. I start too many initiatives such that I cannot possibly maintain all of them well. I try to make too much happen on my own. I am impatient. I'd be a guy flying around the church frantically closing this or that window without thinking. Crash them shut and move along. If I had it my way, I would probably just install an AC unit. Who cares about the cost, the infrastructure of the building itself, or the impact on the aesthetics? Let's control the setting altogether. Let's make something happen for these people. Manufacture an experience. Mass-produce it.

This mentality opposes that of the sacristan who respects God's natural order and the person. The sacristan respected my encounter with God and simply attempted to foster an environment wherein that encounter could occur most peacefully. And he tried to do so without being up on stage, the center of attention. He tried to do so without rushing it. He tried to do so without disturbing things first. He took his time. He cared about God. He cared about me.

Like a Glove: Allowing the Holy Spirit to Act

Ven. Madeleine Delbrêl offers a striking image of the *action* of the Holy Spirit in our lives that is worth reflecting upon. Here's what she says:

> A love like this [i.e., love of witnesses] is a costly, expensive love . . .You have to pray a lot to obtain this love. God does not give the salvation of others to active people but to actions. Not to active people for whom activity is full of bad leavening from our old nature. But to actions, which are a glove of very soft leather on the fingers of the Holy Spirit.[14]

Note that the action or activity she's talking about has nothing to do with a kind of frenetic over-activism or busy-bodiness. This is not the cult of constant activity. She characterizes such activity as being full of bad leaven from our attempts to make things happen on our own—without God. Instead, she's talking about the action of the Holy Spirit and the movement of the Spirit animating our lives. This activity matters.

I would like to offer seven points of reflection on Delbrêl's image:

1. A "hand-in-glove"—this idiom gets at intimacy, deep collaboration, and "the perfect fit." A glove that's too big or too small is annoying, cumbersome. The "fit" of the Holy Spirit into our lives is the perfect fit. It is something deep and intimate.

2. A glove does not move itself but must be moved by the hand that fills and animates it. This is how the Holy Spirit should be in our lives. The Spirit is the animator within us who moves us.

3. A glove manifests the movements of the hand within it. When someone wears a glove, you do not see their hand moving, but the glove. Our lives, too, should show forth the movement of the Holy Spirit. The Spirit, who is invisible, becomes visible through our lives.

14. Delbrêl, *Holiness of Ordinary People*, 47.

4. When wearing a glove, the fingerprints of the hand are on the inside of the glove. The fingerprints of the Holy Spirit are on the interior of our lives—our interior life. The spiritual life is the life in the Spirit. We want the "fingerprints" of the Holy Spirit all over the interior of our lives.

5. Madeleine Delbrêl points out that the glove is *soft* leather. Leather needs to be worn in. Think of new leather shoes or a new baseball glove. That leather is stiff and needs to be worn in, softened. You wear in a baseball glove by applying oil, working it, pounding it with a rubber mallet. You have to work it. The key is, something outside the leather itself has to work on it, move it, bend it. The same is true for us. The Christian life is all about opening up to someone else— God—to be worked on, to be worked in.

6. You often use leather gloves for hard work. Work gloves made of leather allow a person to handle rough and difficult things without damaging or injuring the hands. So too, as Catholic Christians, we are often called to handle tough situations. Really, the Spirit wants to handle the tough situation. Our lives, our actions are simply his glove.

7. However, you can also use a leather glove to handle delicate things. When dealing with a rare jewel or piece of artwork, one uses a gloved hand to not mar the surface of the image in any way. Such items are handled with a certain delicacy. So too with the souls entrusted to our care by God (by this, I mean every person we encounter in any given moment). We are to handle them with delicacy, regardless of how rough they are.

Silence: Clearing the Air

Though they are to be places of prayer, parishes are noisy things. There is a lot of chatter. It's easy to participate in it and for this noise to sweep us away. The world is noisy enough as it is. The computers we carry in our pockets are constant reminders of that. There's no need for the parish to contribute to the cacophony.

Often, parish staff members add to the din. I suppose it's because we're frustrated or dissatisfied. We grumble. This is decently hard work, after all. But that discontent breeds noise. "From the fullness of the heart the mouth speaks" (Luke 6:45). We are prone to grumble. In his *Rule*, a rather short book, St. Benedict discourages grumbling eight times! Constant whining is destructive in the life of a community. It's cancerous. Commenting on St. Benedict's disdain for grumbling, Benedictine monk J. Augustine Wetta explains that "if you think about it, an outright fight is easier on a community than that ceaseless, cowardly, whining gossip that comes from a grumbler who 'spreads strife' and 'separates close friends' (Prov 16:28) . . . Grumbling makes everyone restless and angry—including the grumbler himself."[15]

The discontent that fills the heart does need an outlet, so to speak. That first outlet needs to be prayer, which also includes listening. Blaise Pascal basically said the same thing once: "I have often said that the sole cause of man's unhappiness is that he does not know how to stay quietly in his room."[16] Parishes need agents of silence. Those who, at the core, quiet themselves (internally and externally) and in humble silence seek the God who is silent. Parish staffs need members who embrace silence and so become prophets of silence.

Silence leads to the discovery of God who, though Other, dwells within. Earlier I quoted Robert Cardinal Sarah on this: "At the heart of man there is an innate silence, for God abides in the innermost part of every person. God is silence, and this divine silence dwells in man."[17] Parishes need people, staff people, who are capable of silence and who discover God in it—then show that way of silence and presence to others.

---

15. Wetta, *Humility Rules*, 68–69.

16. Pascal, *Pensées*, 37.

17. Sarah, *Power of Silence*, 22.

Discern: Getting the Question Right

As a melancholic prone to melancholic fits, I often found myself discouraged as I left the parish late each Sunday night. No matter how many "successes" I could point to following a youth ministry event, nothing could shake me from my gloom. After meandering through this weekly dejection for several years, the Lord answered my prayer one Sunday night as I begged for help. As I made my three-minute commute, the Lord spoke swiftly and with stunning force. His words were not accusatory. They were simply true. He let me know I was asking my team the wrong question.

See, at the end of each youth night, I would gather my core team of volunteer adults. We would debrief and pray. Usually, I would open the dialogue with this query: "How do you think that went?" And, usually, one or two positive comments would be followed by a negative one about the timing of the schedule, some sloppily run aspect of the meeting, or a dismal small group session. And this one negative comment would be followed by several (or many) others until our time ran out and we prayed a "Hail Mary" and left . . . dejected.

I was asking the wrong question. In the final analysis, do our thoughts about "success" or "failure" in ministry matter much at all? If this is the Lord's work, then what matters most is what he did and how he spoke.

I started asking a new question: "What was God doing tonight?" This one question changed everything. Now, we prayed differently before events—with openness and expectant faith. During events, my team paid more attention to the activity of the Holy Spirit and to those finer details of ministry that are often missed. Meetings ended not with time for input (though sometimes this was necessary for logistical or pastoral purposes), but with testimony. The air of negativity vaporized. The grumbling was gone.

Eventually we took another step and turned the testimony into a prayer of thanksgiving: "What should we thank God for tonight?" At this point, we had moved out of the format of a debriefing meeting and into a moment of prayer. Our events always began and ended with prayer, but now they ended with a more mature expression of prayer.

Seeking to give testimony over and above input radically changed our debriefing meetings, and it also changed our other meetings (e.g., monthly planning meetings). The more attentive we were to the activity of the Holy Spirit as a leadership community in our communal discernment and testimony, the more attentive we were to the Lord's will for next steps in ministry.

Prune: Chopping Block

As fallen human beings, marred by a certain distrust of God and forgetfulness of his providence, we tend to attach inordinately to things or relationships or reputation or power. The list goes on and on. In ministry, the temptation to form similar attachments prowls about every parish or chancery. We can get fixated on certain relationships, certain ways of doing things, and certain programs. Again, the list goes on and on. We exert tremendous energy building structures for the communication of the gospel, but then we often start idolizing those structures. We forget that the project or the program or whatever it is exists for the sake of Christ and not for ourselves.

I can't quite remember when my group of youth minister friends started doing this, but we put all our shared ministry efforts in the crucible each year. Following a year of ministry, we would meet for prayer, discussion, and discernment. We would evaluate each of the ministries or programs on which we had collaborated. What was the good fruit? What was the bad? What needs to be adjusted for next year? What needs to be pruned?

Then, after analyzing each of them, we'd take a step back and ask a more radical series question: Is God asking us to offer each of these again next year? Or, is God asking us to do something different? Are there groups of teens we are currently not serving, but we're being called to serve? Are we pooling too many resources in one area that has proven to be minimally fruitful even though it logically seems like the right thing? Are we doing something just because a few people like it, or we don't want to hurt someone's feelings? Do we need to take the axe to the root of one or more of our programs?

Eventually we referred to this process as "the chopping block." The chopping block was a way to collectively detach from each part of the ministry (because forming inordinate attachments is a real thing!) and to open ourselves once again to the freshness of the Holy Spirit—the God who makes all things new (cf. Rev 21:5).

The depth of our friendship allowed us to engage in such a daring exercise. We had built up a vulnerability-based trust over the years and it became palpable in the chopping block meeting each year. Since then, I've been able to take this practice to other teams I've led, but always trying to introduce it at the right time and when enough trust has been built up. I also know I have to lead by example. This means putting my own projects down on the block first.

Friendship: Ministering as Disciple-Friends

In her essay "The Generation of Saints," Sherry A. Weddell describes the Catholic revival in France following the Protestant Reformation. The precise details of how the revival emerged are not the focus of her reflection. Instead, she emphasizes that the real drivers of the revival were "disciple-friends." "Thousands were actively involved in the renewal," Weddell says, "but the major figures included a cardinal, a bishop, three priests . . . two young widows with children, a Parisian housewife, a single woman, a professional soldier, and a shoemaker. Today, the same group is recognized for including four canonized saints, two blesseds, one Doctor of the Church, and six founders of religious congregations."[18] Not too shabby.

The diversity of characters and states in life is kind of incredible. But, the most incredible thing is the power of friendship. Weddell characterizes this particular group as being one of "disciple-friends." These friends were also disciples. They were

18. Weddell, "Generation of Saints," 12–13.

growing in friendship with God. And, as they were moving towards him, they encountered others who were being drawn to the same Source. They became friends and their friendship supported this movement toward God. The friendship also became magnetic, attracting others to the Source of the friendship.

As I reflect on fifteen years of ministry, I can confidently say that the most fruitful ministry was born of friendship. Friendship is one of those intangibles in ministry. It can't be taught or forced or anything like that. It just kind of happens and *one needs to be open to it happening.*

Surrender: Praying When Nothing Seems to Work

What do you do when ministerial hustle isn't working? What do you do when the person you're building relationship with flakes or heads down a bad path? What do you do when things are falling apart, a teen is stuck in the wrong crowd, or an adult you're walking with becomes nonresponsive?

You hustle some more.

Another text message. A phone call. Fasting. The Rosary.

All of it.

And, when that doesn't seem to be working?

This was the topic of a conversation between me and a friend several years into my tenure as a parish youth minister. We were recounting a certain spiritual suffering that anyone who is entrusted with the spiritual well-being of people experiences as those people take divergent paths. Recently, he had taken another step in his journey. When the hustling didn't work, he went straight to adoration. In front of the Eucharist, he imagined himself handing over the teen (in this case) to Jesus at the cross. In this way, he was uniting that spiritual pain with that of Christ on the cross, while rightfully entrusting the person in need to Jesus.

This act of surrender, it seems to me, is the right move *all the time.* In other words, it doesn't have to be part of a last-ditch effort after our attempts at hustling fail. Making this a regular spiritual practice helps us to avoid the temptation that our hustling might be the cause of certain successes in ministry, rather than seeing that any positive movement in disciple-making results from God and God alone—not our efforts, however great or small they might be.

Making this act of surrender before a crucifix or in eucharistic adoration is powerful. To take it a step further: *the* time and place to make such acts of abandonment and entrustment is during offertory at Mass. Here, we bring before the Lord and spiritually place on the altar that which we are offering. We surrender it all to him.

Sacrifice: Making an Offering for the Other

Occasionally, you read something that makes you put a book down and take a deep breath. Like a really deep one. This happened to me once when I read the following passage from Joseph Ratzinger:

> The last and highest mission of the Church in relation to non-believers is to suffer for them and in their place as the Master did. At the end of his life, only a few days before his Passion, Christ described his life's mission in these words: "The Son of Man came not to be served but to serve, and to give his love as a ransom for many" (Mark 10:45). These words express not only Christ's own life, but the basic law of all Christian discipleship. The disciples of Christ will always be "few," as the Lord said, and as such stand before the mass, the "many," as Jesus, the one, stands before the many (that is, the whole of mankind) . . . The disciples of Jesus are few, but as Jesus himself was one "for the many," so it will always be their mission to be not against but "for the many." When all other ways fail, there will always remain the royal way of vicarious suffering by the side of the Lord. It is in her defeat that the Church constantly achieves her highest victory and stands nearest to Christ . . . Seen in this way, the relationship between the "few" and the "many" reveals the true measure of the Church's catholicity. In external numbers it will never be fully "catholic" (that is, all embracing), but will always remain a small flock . . . In her suffering and love, however, she will always stand

for the "many," for all. In her love and her suffering she surmounts all frontiers and is truly "catholic."[19]

Ministering from the inside out primes one for a kind of vicarious suffering, because it means ministering from the heart of Christ—the one who suffered "for the many." This is the plain truth: sometimes ministry just hurts. Sometimes, things fail or people leave. One can become bitter or discouraged. Or one can embrace that suffering for what it is and offer it in union with Christ. That trite Catholic imperative does get at a foundational truth: "offer it up." When we do, when we offer our joys and pains, our frustrations and hurts, in union with Jesus and "for the many," it's then that we enter most deeply into the mystical core of evangelization.

19. Ratzinger, *Meaning of Christian Brotherhood*, 83–84.

— 5 —

Healing

E arly in my time of ministry, I heard the expression "the surest way to lose your faith is to work for the Church." Initially, I thought it was ridiculous. I was zealous and youthful. I loved Jesus. Surely, I would buck the trend and make it through unscathed. But, after ten years, it was starting to happen. I was jaded. I was also losing faith in the Church, which means I was also losing faith in Jesus Christ who founded her. You see a lot of the church's humanity when you "work for the Church." It's unappetizing. And it's difficult to eat Church sausage after seeing how it's made. That's the bottom line.

Jadedness sets in slowly and over time. It lies under the surface, infecting thoughts, feelings, and desires like a cancer. One day, for whatever reason, you finally diagnose it: "I'm jaded." Or someone else diagnoses it for you. Once, my brother-in-law was sharing about a recent hire in an archdiocesan office and some of the hope he had for the impact the position could have. I listened. Then, without hesitation, I unloaded. I went off about how the position would amount to nothing, how people would tear it down from the inside, how it would get caught up in bureaucratic red tape. He listened patiently. Then, he said, "Wow. You *really* are jaded." It stung. He was right.

The origins of one's jadedness vary, and the experience is quite personal. The causes for a person's becoming jaded could be tied to sin, scandal (every sin committed by one member of the church against another is a scandal), being wounded by another Church worker (i.e., sin), bureaucratic machinations, analysis paralysis, ministry monotony, overwork, disorganization, poor administration and leadership, and the sense of futility that comes from working in an organization that sometimes feels a bit like being on a rather large sinking ship in the north Atlantic.

As I reflect on my own jadedness, I see that it has less to do with being burnt out from doing a lot of stuff and more to do with people in the Church who have hurt me along the way. Most of the jaded people I know have been worn down more than worn out. They're calloused and wounded. Rather, they're calloused because they're wounded. Jadedness is the festering of wounds that haven't healed, wounds on top of wounds. Infected wounds. Scar tissue. You get the picture.

I can also see how I got idealistic about the Church. This is my Achilles heel. I'm a perfectionist. An idealist. It's easy to project this perfectionism onto the Church. Flannery O'Connor once railed against this kind of ecclesial perfectionism:

> What you seem actually to demand is that the Church put the Kingdom of Heaven on Earth right here now, that the Holy Ghost be translated at once into all flesh. The Holy Spirit very rarely shows himself on the surface of anything. You are asking that man return at once to the state God created him in, you are leaving out the terrible radical human pride that causes death. Christ was crucified on earth and the Church is crucified in time, and the Church is crucified by all of us, by her members most particularly because she is a Church of sinners.[1]

Turns out, the Church is made up of sinners who can sin *real good*. So, it's easy to harbor resentment. It's easy to distrust people. To get political. To become jaded. To be scandalized.

---

1. O'Connor, *Habit of Being*, 307.

Sin is a stumbling block. It's a stumbling block in our own lives and it's a stumbling block for the Church. Being sinned against by another member of the Church, whether that person is a priest, religious, or lay person, is scandalous. And, when I sin against another member of the Church, it is scandalous. J. R. R. Tolkien once said, "I think I am as sensitive as you (or any other Christian) to the 'scandals,' both of clergy and laity. I have suffered grievously in my own life from stupid, tired, dimmed, and even bad priests."[2] That gets at it well, I'd say. The Church is made up of sinners. *Lumen gentium* explains the reality this way: "While Christ, holy, innocent and undefiled knew nothing of sin, but came to expiate only the sins of the people, the Church, embracing in its bosom sinners, at the same time holy and always in need of being purified, always follows the way of penance and renewal."[3]

The Desire for Healing

My basic point, thus far, is this: jadedness signals sickness. It is a symptom of a deeper illness. You get over sickness, not by distraction, but by a healing process. When you're sick, you can distract yourself all you want, you can tell yourself you're not sick, you can try to push through, but you're still sick. The sickness itself, known by the symptoms manifested, needs to be addressed for healing to happen.

We should pause here and note that if one wants to move past this illness, the jaded person must desire healing. Without this desire, and then, without acting on it, nothing will change. One must first admit he or she is jaded. I had to admit it. After having seen jaded priests and lay people for years and vowing to never become jaded, I had become jaded. It hurt to admit this, but it was true. It was humbling.

But humility is the starting point. Humility literally means "on the ground," (from the Latin word *humus*—earth). The path

2. Tolkien, "Letter to Michael Tolkien" (dated November 1, 1963), 474-75.
3. Second Vatican Council, *Lumen gentium*, §8.

HEALING

to being raised up by God out of the pit of boredom begins from this point—humbly admitting to yourself, to God, and to your superiors or your spouse, that you're jaded. The *Catechism* reminds us, referencing Luke 18:9–14, that "He who humbles himself will be exalted; humility is the foundation of prayer." Humility is the foundation of prayer, and prayer marks the path out of jadedness. The journey of spiritual recovery goes by way of prayer, and "only when we humbly acknowledge that 'we do not know how to pray as we ought,' are we ready to receive freely the gift of prayer. 'Man is a beggar before God'" (CCC §2559).

"I can't imagine what it would be like to be free. The thought of it actually frightens me." At first blush, these words from Mary, a woman struggling with an eating disorder, might sound ridiculous. But, Fr. Dave Pivonka, who recounts them in his book *Spiritual Freedom*, points out that it's a common position. Those who are bound "have become so accustomed to their slavery," he says, "that they are not certain they can live without it."[4]

A life of freedom, a life of peace, is a *new* life, an *unknown* life. We bind ourselves to what's comfortable. And, for many of us in ministry, jadedness has become comfortable. It's the norm. The thought of letting it go frightens us. You hear this in our complaints. We complain when nothing changes; we gripe when things do change. The jaded person is never happy. We're afraid of the freedom that will result from being healed of our jadedness, because it's a freedom we haven't tasted in a long, long time. We're afraid of being happy in ministry again.

For those who want to heal, however, the remaining pages of this chapter will provide a few helpful steps, or spiritual exercises, to begin the process of becoming un-jaded.[5]

---

4. Pivonka, *Spiritual Freedom*,

5. To be sure, the remaining points in this chapter can also help one avoid becoming jaded. They are just as preventative as they are reparative.

75

Jadedness and the Calloused Heart

Survival in ministry requires a certain thickness of skin. I suppose being thick-skinned has something to do with nature. Some people are naturally thick-skinned. Others are "nurtured" into it. Experience and learning how to deal with challenging circumstances and criticism thickens one's personality. For most people, some combination of natural disposition and experience thickens the skin.

For the jaded person, thick skin becomes hard, calloused skin. Jadedness manifests a kind of disregard for others, an apathy, an insensitivity. Bitterness. In short, jadedness results in a kind of hardness of heart. The heart becomes calloused. Typically, one hardens his or her heart as a self-defense mechanism. The heart defends itself against further hurt or disappointment. Resentment and fear take over. Jadedness and hardness of heart go hand in hand. So, what can penetrate the calloused heart?

Steps toward Healing

The path to healing for the jaded church worker moves from the inside out. The trajectory of this book, from rootedness in identity and the interior life, to investing in one's primary vocation and its overflow into ministry—this trajectory marks something of a road to recovery. Yet jadedness may require further healing and conversion. The following, though not exhaustive, offers several concrete steps I have taken to work through my own jadedness.

Shift the Mentality

Frustrated by the bog of diocesan bureaucracy, I asked him point blank: "How have you been a priest for so long and you're not jaded?" He looked at me, collecting himself.

The retired monsignor was an anomaly in my mind. As a lay worker in the Church, I had encountered countless worn-out priests, deacons, and lay people. I sensed none of their boredom and apathy in him. He was not jaded.

I broke the silence and set the question before the wise priest once again: "How is it that you're not jaded?" He answered:

> You know, there have been moments as I've been drawn to the center [meaning, the center of the Church's institutional structures]. I got curious. I wanted to be "in." The closer I got to the center, it was then and there that I could feel that sense of jadedness coming on. During one of those times of becoming jaded, I realized that I don't work for the Church. This whole ministry thing isn't a purely human thing. I don't *work* for the Church. This is the wrong way of seeing it. Instead, I am on mission with Christ.

A "working-for-the-Church" mentality can lead to a lot of navel-gazing. There's a self-indulgent criticism about everything. Constant grumbling. I mean, navels are not that pretty. You hear this negative talk nearly everywhere Church workers gather—planning meetings, the sacristy, the front desk, and so forth. In these ecclesiocentric environs, Church things orbit around themselves and one forgets what Christianity is all about. We get caught up in the endless flood of trifling affairs. In all honesty, everything "churchy" starts to look and sound terrible after a while.

But to say, "I am on mission with Christ" is to orient oneself toward Another and others. There's no wallowing here. Instead, one looks to Christ and those at whom he's looking. This is about participating in mission and ministry and seeing them for what they are—theandric activities. In other words, they are initiated by God who invites our participation in them. They are not contrived by humans and carried out with their own devices (and frustrations, politics, and so forth).

Madeleine Delbrêl takes all this a step further. She says the "method is not to work for Christ but to relive Christ in the midst of a de-Christianized world." Beyond being on mission with Christ, Delbrêl says we are to become Christ. To relive Christ is to become Christ, to be Christ. To become who we are, as Christians, this is the goal. Consequently, we need to "be acted upon, not to act."[6] God is the one who acts, who moves. God is the one who fashions us into Christ. We receive and respond.

A Church on mission with her spouse, a Church becoming one with and identifying with her spouse, is the better and more Christocentric way to think about ministry. It's a mental antidote to that jadedness lurking about at every turn.

Make a Retreat

Retreats are so important that Canon Law says priests "are equally bound to make time for spiritual retreats according to prescripts of particular law" (Can 276.2.4). It goes on. "[Religious] are faithfully to observe the period of annual retreat" (Can 663 §5). Oh, and we cannot forget about seminarians: "Each year [seminarians] are to make a spiritual retreat" (Can 246 §5).

Interestingly, there's no prescription for lay people. No mention about paid time off for the lay minister to go on a weeklong retreat. No talk of an allowance to help cover childcare. A lay person in ministry must forge his or her own path in this case.

Admittedly, I've not done a good job with this. In ministry, I tend to lead so many events that take me away from the family during evenings and weekends that the thought of leaving them again for my own retreat has always been hard to stomach. It feels selfish and inconsiderate. I'm ashamed to admit it, but in all the years of doing ministry, I've only taken one personal retreat. Now, I've organized retreat days for lay ministers, but whenever you're organizing anything, you're not retreating.

So, it seems I have little to say about a personal retreat. But, I will say what I can: That one personal retreat I have taken was tremendously fruitful. I could think more clearly and I had an opportunity to unburden my heart in prayer and the sacraments. I was able to drink deep in the spiritual life and in the grace God had for me. It was clear, very early on in my retreat, that a personal retreat has incredible value. It is necessary to avoid burnout and

6. Delbrêl, *Holiness of Ordinary People*, 19.

jadedness. It's also helpful when it comes to healing jadedness. At least it was for me.

Now, let's go back to the problem the married lay person has: the circumstantial difficulty of springing for a retreat. This can be solved in one of two ways. On the one hand, you simply make it a priority. It's so important that it's worth the cost to your spouse and your children. Obviously, this decision has to be made in union with your spouse. On the other hand, and this is typically my strategy, you take mini-retreats within your normal circumstances.

My ministry schedule has always been flexible and I don't usually have a supervisor breathing down my neck (thanks be to God). It's not uncommon, therefore, for me to take a half-day or even a full day, and retreat. You might find me at a local shrine or retreat center, or at daily Mass and then at a coffee shop to read or journal. I can make the most of pretty much any set of circumstances. Getting away, getting out of the office, away from the daily grind, that is key. These retreats carved out of my ministry schedule can happen with some frequency throughout the year. And, doing it while my kids are at school is a great bonus.

Forgive

We all know the most haunting line of the Our Father: "Forgive us our trespasses as we forgive those who trespass against us." The degree to which we forgive, well, that's the degree to which we'll be forgiven by God. In Matthew's Gospel, Jesus says, "If you forgive others their transgressions, your heavenly Father will forgive you" (Matt 6:14). When Peter asks how often one must forgive, Jesus says, "Seventy-seven times" (Matt 18:22). This is a symbolic number representing a never-ending way that we ought to forgive.

This rocks most jaded people (myself included), because harboring resentment is a key ingredient. But if you want healing for jadedness, you most likely need to forgive others.

What is forgiveness? Forgiveness is basically my free decision—it cannot be forced—to see the other person as a person again. Instead of seeing the other as a non-person, the cause of my hurt, the sum of their faults, etc., I make an act of the will, a choice, to see the other first and foremost as another human person. Forgiving the other does not mean excusing or implicitly condoning the wrongful action as "okay." Forgiving the other does not mean that the pain caused by the offense vanishes, nor does it mean one should stuff away feelings or suppress memories.

Forgiveness justly acknowledges the truth by acknowledging the wrong as wrong. But it does not stop there. Forgiveness is an act of mercy springing from the depths of one's heart, the depths that have first been touched by God's merciful initiative. Forgiveness means completely giving the other his or her personhood again. In other words, forgiveness restores the possibility of a relationship where the relationship had been damaged or destroyed, and invites a path for ongoing healing, rebuilding trust, and so forth.

Forgiveness is, obviously, difficult. It's hard because it means exposing the heart. It tears down walls of resentment; it pierces hardness of heart and opens the heart to the risk of love once again. The arduousness of forgiveness cannot be denied. I once spoke with a priest about this, and he invited me to turn acts of forgiveness into a prayer. Said another way, he challenged me to invoke God's help in forgiving others. He gave me simple words to which I've had recourse countless times over the years. The prayer formula goes like this:

"I forgive _____ (name of person), for _____ (what the person did), in the name of the Father, and of the Son, and of the Holy Spirit." Then, take a deep breath and listen.

I repeat this as often as necessary, which is to say, quite often.

Reconcile

Jesus asks us to forgive. This is a non-negotiable in the Christian life. He goes further, however, and calls for the restoration of the relationship whenever possible. Jesus says, "If you bring your gift to the altar, and there recall that your brother has anything against you, leave your gift there at the altar, go first and be reconciled with your brother, and then come and offer your gift" (Matt 5:23–24).

Forgiveness opens the opportunity for relationship; reconciliation brings it about. Reconciliation heals relationships.

Now, in some cases, reconciliation may be impossible (e.g., with the deceased) or imprudent (e.g., in the case of abuse). However, in many cases, it is possible. But this doesn't mean it's easy. In fact, it's intensely humbling to admit fault or to correct someone else's fault. And, as we know, most issues involve both parties, so both people need to humble themselves to be reconciled. And, in our digitized and distracted culture, most conflict gets brushed under the rug and people pick up their phones for a good doomscroll. In ministry (and life in general), when we don't confront conflict and seek resolution and reconciliation, resentment sets in quickly. Walls go up and persons suffer—and ministry suffers. And, well, people build a foundation for jadedness. There's nothing worse than a parish office full of hurt, jaded people laden with resentment.

So, how can someone in ministry be reconciled with another?

I think the process can be rather straightforward. If I perceive that I have wronged a person, I can simply take ownership of my fault and responsibility for reconciling by saying something like the following: "I apologize for _____ (whatever I did), and it was wrong. Will you forgive me?"

Let's examine these words for a moment. Notice the admission of fault renames the offense—it puts flesh back on the sin. I have to state, clearly, what I did. And, not only that, I must admit that it was wrong. I think this is the key. It's not just saying "sorry" as in "excuse me." This formula requires a clear statement of the offense and an admission that it was morally wrong. Then, and only then, do I ask for forgiveness. This process provokes the freedom of the injured party. Only that person can *freely* say "I forgive you." From here, we can continue our path of reconciliation by talking through how we will approach similar situations in the future to not damage the relationship again.

I believe reconciliation on any team is critical for good ministry. It's essential, really. Relationships at the heart of ministry have to remain healthy—or get healthy. Healing relationships, and healing jaded hearts, usually requires a path of forgiveness and reconciliation (whenever possible).

Now, I'm neither naive nor idealistic. I know sometimes reconciliation simply doesn't work. In certain cases, people just don't work well together and relationships become irreparable. However, this fact does not absolve us from trying to reconcile—to risk reconciliation, so to speak.

Soften the Calloused Heart

When it comes to healing the calloused heart, I've found memory to be key. I would like to develop this thought with two points. First, remembering the joy of one's encounter (or encounters) with the Lord helps to soften the heart. I have found it to be most effective to spend time before the Blessed Sacrament in eucharistic adoration considering the events leading up to encountering Christ, the encounter itself, and what happened afterwards. It is even helpful to consider what my life could look like had God not met me at particular time and place. Sometimes I try to take a pilgrimage of sorts, returning to the physical places of encounter. For me, this is a Marian shrine near my hometown or a return trip to Franciscan University of Steubenville.

Second, most people who have done ministry for a while hold on to hurtful memories and harbor resentment as a result of these hurts. This is that callousness I'm talking about. These hurts haunt us. The memories sting. As painful as this sounds, I find it helpful to spend time in adoration considering those hurtful memories—inviting God to show me where he was within the particular situation.

This is not magic. Sometimes, I don't perceive or hear anything in prayer. God's presence in a particular scene in my life remains a mystery. However, I find as I continue offering the instance to God, surrendering to him my hardness of heart that resulted from it, quite often the picture becomes clearer and I get a sense of what he was up to in his providential allowance of something. Almost without fail, I gain insight into the person (or persons) who hurt me, and I can feel myself growing in compassion.

Confess

The Sacrament of Reconciliation is a powerful antidote to jaded-ness. In fact, the Sacrament of Reconciliation does far more than allow the contrite sinner to experience forgiveness. That forgiveness leads to reconciliation, and reconciliation to healing. The *Catechism* says as much: "God's forgiveness initiates the healing," and "the sinner is healed" (§1502 and §1448, respectively).

Finding a regular confessor, a priest to whom you go for the sacrament with some frequency, can be helpful here. A regular confessor can get to know you, learn more of your story and those "near occasions of sin," and offer better pastoral advice with this clearer window into the situation. From my experience, no priest has ever turned down my request for regular confession (usually monthly), and it has always been a blessing.

Long Live Good Humor

When it comes to jadedness in ministry, one can be sure it is not of the Lord. Joylessness is not of God. On this point, Ratzinger argues that God's gift reigns where joy exists, and, conversely, "where joylessness rules and humor dies, we may be certain that the Holy Spirit, the Spirit of Jesus Christ, is not present."[7] In other words, it's okay to laugh and to enjoy ministry, oh jaded soul! May the Holy Spirit soften our hardened and calloused hearts, again and again. Come, Holy Spirit.

7. Ratzinger, *God of Jesus Christ*, 113.

Conclusion

I would like to conclude this little book with the passage I read and pray with most often:

> I am the true vine, and my Father is the vine grower. He takes away every branch in me that does not bear fruit, and every one that does he prunes so that it bears more fruit. You are already pruned because of the word that I spoke to you. Remain in me, as I remain in you. Just as a branch cannot bear fruit on its own unless it remains on the vine, so neither can you unless you remain in me. I am the vine, you are the branches. Whoever remains in me and I in him will bear much fruit, because without me you can do nothing. (John 15:1–5)

Jesus spoke these words right after instituting the Eucharist. As those disciples sat in eucharistic amazement, Jesus tells them that he is the vine and they are the branches. He is going to prune them so they bear more fruit. He's going to prune us, too. May we be open to such pruning!

Note the preposition "in." Remain *in* me; I remain *in* you. Remember, they had just received Jesus' real presence, Jesus himself, in their bodies. He is "in" them. Simultaneously, the Eucharist makes us into him. How? Pope Benedict XVI explains this mystery by quoting Augustine. In the person of the Eucharist, Augustine says, "I am the food of grown men; grow, and you shall feed upon me; nor shall you change me, like the food of your flesh, into yourself, but you shall be changed into me." Benedict XVI explains, "It is not the eucharistic food that is changed into us, but rather we who are mysteriously transformed by it. Christ nourishes us by uniting us to himself; 'he draws us into himself.'"[1] The Eucharist is that "superfood," that "wonderbread" that works in the opposite way of normal food. Rather than being transformed into us, absorbed into our bodies, we are conformed to and transformed into Jesus. In this way, in this eucharistic way, we abide, we remain *in* him. Abiding *in* the Eucharist is the key to living from the *in*-side out.

Then, we have this final line. Without Christ, without the Eucharist, we can do nothing. It doesn't say, "without me you can do a few things" or "without me you can do something." Jesus says you can do *nothing*. Such words should probably be tattooed on the brains of church workers, because we try to do things on our own and with our own devices all the time.

When we try to do things on our own, we're bound to sink. We capsize in our primary vocations and plunge our interior lives into the darkness of the abyss. And so, as a final word, I will leave us with St. Augustine's reflection on Jesus' warning about trying to do anything without him:

> If you have any sense remaining, let your hair stand on end. For whoever imagines that he is bearing fruit of himself is not in the vine, and he that is not in the vine is not in Christ, and he that is not in Christ is not a Christian. Such are the ocean depths into which you have plunged.[2]

---

1. Benedict XVI, *Sacramentum Caritatis*, §70.
2. Augustine of Hippo, "Tractate 81."

Action Plan for Living from the Inside Out

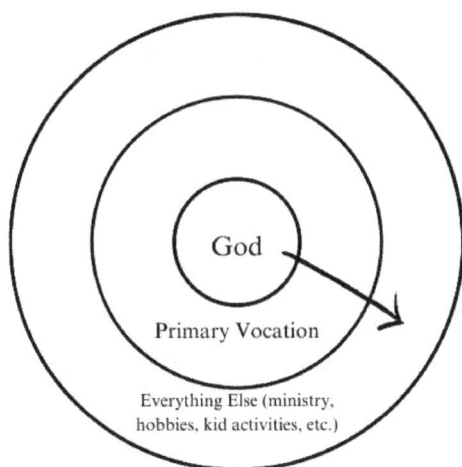

For the adopted son or daughter of God, life from the inside out means living securely rooted in Jesus Christ.

The Fundamentals of Life from the Inside Out

- Core Identity: To live securely as God's adopted son or daughter means claiming and embracing one's baptismal identity.

- Interior Life: We abide in our identity by entering more and more deeply into the sacramental life of the Church and into an interior life of intimate, personal prayer.

- Primary Vocation: We are called to be faithful to our state in life and generous within it. We encounter God's love in a concrete way in our vocational state, which also serves as the primary "space" in which we exercise charity.

- Generous Ministry: God's grace flows from the interior life and through one's vocation to fill the life of ministry. Ministry is always most fruitful when it is led by the Spirit in a community of persons devoted to Christ and leading others to him.

Note: Wounds fester. Resentment builds. Sometimes we need to avail ourselves to God's deeper healing as a necessary first (and enduring) step to living from the inside out.

Action Plan Worksheet

Step 1: Reflect

Guided by the Holy Spirit, identify an area of desired growth from the list of fundamentals above. In what area might God be calling you to grow? Why?

Step 2: Aim

Keep the end in mind. What good fruit do you hope to see? How will you know you are growing in this particular area? How will growth in this area allow you to give of yourself more wholly and fruitfully? Be clear and specific.

Step 3: Learn

Note any knowledge or content source(s) that can "inform" and "inspire" growth in the area you chose. For example, spiritual reading, podcasts, programs, and so forth.

Step 4: Strategize

List the practical steps you will take to pursue the desired growth. Set goals.

Step 5: Account

What support or accountability do you need to help you pursue this growth? Who can you call on to hold you accountable for your goals?

Step 6: Persevere

Set a realistic timeline for working with the Holy Spirit towards this growth in holiness. How long will you focus on this particular area of desired growth? Remain faithful to that commitment.

Step 7: Beg

Ask God (repeatedly) for the grace to follow through on your commitments, that he might bring to completion the good work he has begun in you (cf. Phil 1:6).

Bibliography

XIII Ordinary General Assembly of the Synod of Bishops. *Lineamenta: The New Evangelization for the Transmission of the Christian Faith*. Vatican City: Libreria Editrice Vaticana, 2011.

Augustine of Hippo. "Tractate 81." Translated by John Gibb. From *Nicene and Post-Nicene Fathers, First Series*, vol. 7. Edited by Philip Schaff. Buffalo, NY: Christian Literature, 1888. Revised and edited for New Advent by Kevin Knight. http://www.newadvent.org/fathers/1701081.htm.

Balthasar, Hans Urs Von. *Razing the Bastions: On the Church in This Age*. Translated by Brian McNeil. San Francisco: Ignatius, 1993.

Benedict XVI. "Benedict XVI General Audience Address of April 12, 2011— The Holiness." Citta del Vaticano: Libreria Editrice Vaticana, 2011.

———. "Homily—May 3, 2009." Citta del Vaticano: Libreria Editrice Vaticana, 2009.

———. *Jesus of Nazareth: From the Baptism in the Jordan to the Transfiguration*. Translated by Adrian J. Walker. New York: Doubleday, 2007.

———. "Meditation During the First General Congregation." Citta del Vaticano: Libreria Editrice Vaticana, 2012.

———. *Sacramentum Caritatis*. Citta del Vaticano: Libreria Editrice Vaticana, 2007.

———. *Verbum Domini*. Citta del Vaticano: Libreria Editrice Vaticana, 2010.

———. *Western Culture: Today and Tomorrow*. Translated by Michael J. Miller. San Francisco: Ignatius, 2019.

Chautard, Jean-Baptiste. *The Soul of the Apostolate*. Translated by a Monk of Our Lady of Gethsemani. London: Catholic Way, 2014.

Code of Canon Law: Latin-English Edition. Washington, DC: Canon Law Society of America, 1999.

Cummings, Charles. *Monastic Practices*. Kalamazoo, MI: Cistercian, 1986.

Delbrêl, Madeleine. *The Holiness of Ordinary People*. Edited by Gilles François and Bernard Pitaud. Translated by Mary Dudro Gordon and Abigail Tardiff. San Francisco: Ignatius, 2024.

Douglas, Harper. "Etymology of Jade." Online Etymology Dictionary. Accessed June 29, 2024. https://www.etymonline.com/word/jade#etymonline_v_42714.

Guardini, Romano. *The Spirit of the Liturgy*. Translated by Ada Lane. New York: Aeterna, 2015.

Hayden, Robert. "Those Winter Sundays." In *Collected Poems of Robert Hayden*, edited by Frederick Glaysher, 41. London: Liveright, 1985.

John Paul II. *Christifideles Laici*. Citta del Vaticano: Libreria Editrice Vaticana, 1988.

———. "Homily—17th World Youth Day (July 28, 2002)." Citta del Vaticano: Libreria Editrice Vaticana, 2002.

Johnson, Dan, dir. *My Father's Father*. Season 1, episode 1, "A Good Father." Franciscan University: Faith & Reason. https://faithandreason.com/series/my-fathers-father/.

Kreeft, Peter. *Prayer for Beginners*. San Francisco: Ignatius, 2000.

Mallon, James. *Divine Renovation*. New London, CT: Twenty-Third, 2014.

McLeod, Saul. "Attachment Theory in Psychology." Simply Psychology. https://www.simplypsychology.org/attachment.html#.

Nouwen, Henri. *The Return of the Prodigal Son*. New York: Image, 1992.

O'Connor, Flannery. *The Habit of Being*. New York: Farrar, Straus and Giroux, 1988.

Pascal, Blaise. *Pensées*. Translated by A. J. Krailsheimer. New York: Penguin, 1995.

Paul VI. *Evangelii nuntiandi*. Citta del Vaticano: Libreria Editrice Vaticana, 1975.

Philippe, Jacques. *Searching for and Maintaining Peace: A Small Treatise on Peace of Heart*. Translated by George and Jannic Driscoll. New York: St. Paul's, 2002.

Pivonka, Dave. *Spiritual Freedom: God's Life-changing Gift*. Cincinnati: Franciscan Media, 2008.

Ratzinger, Joseph. *Behold the Pierced One*. Translated by Graham Harrison. San Francisco: Ignatius, 1986.

———. *Pilgrim Fellowship of Faith*. Translated by Henry Taylor. San Francisco: Ignatius, 2005.

———. *The God of Jesus Christ*. Translated by Brian McNeil. San Francisco: Ignatius, 2008.

———. *The Meaning of Christian Brotherhood*. San Francisco: Ignatius, 1993.

———. *The Yes of Jesus Christ*. Translated by Robert Nowell. New York: Crossroad, 1991.

Sarah, Robert. *The Power of Silence*. Translated by Michael J. Miller. San Francisco: Ignatius, 2017.

Scanlan, Michael. *Appointment with God*. Steubenville, OH: Franciscan University Press, 1987.

Second Vatican Council. *Lumen gentium.* Vatican City: Libreria Editrice Vaticano, 1964

Tolkien, J. R. R. "Letter 250: To Michael Tolkien." In *The Letters of J. R. R. Tolkien: Revised and Expanded Edition,* edited by Humphrey Carpenter and Christopher Tolkien, 472–78. New York: William Morrow, 2023.

Verner, Dominic. "The Tears of St. Dominic." *Dominica,* September 23, 2011. https://www.dominicajournal.org/the-tears-of-saint-dominic/.

Weddell, Sherry A. "The Generation of Saints." In *Becoming a Parish of Intentional Disciples,* edited by Sherry A. Weddell, 11–28. Huntington, IN: Our Sunday Visitor, 2015.

Wetta, J. Augustine. *Humility Rules: St. Benedict's Twelve Step Guide to Genuine Self-Esteem.* San Francisco: Ignatius, 2017.